Jimmy Rolando Molina Ríos
Ronald Christopher Elizalde López
Salviano Vicente Núñez Apolo

Quality Metrics

Jimmy Rolando Molina Ríos
Ronald Christopher Elizalde López
Salviano Vicente Núñez Apolo

Quality Metrics

ISO/IEC 9126 - ISO/IEC 25000 - ISO/IEC 14598

ScienciaScripts

Imprint
Any brand names and product names mentioned in this book are subject to trademark, brand or patent protection and are trademarks or registered trademarks of their respective holders. The use of brand names, product names, common names, trade names, product descriptions etc. even without a particular marking in this work is in no way to be construed to mean that such names may be regarded as unrestricted in respect of trademark and brand protection legislation and could thus be used by anyone.

Cover image: www.ingimage.com

This book is a translation from the original published under ISBN 978-613-9-44044-3.

Publisher:
Sciencia Scripts
is a trademark of
Dodo Books Indian Ocean Ltd. and OmniScriptum S.R.L publishing group

120 High Road, East Finchley, London, N2 9ED, United Kingdom
Str. Armeneasca 28/1, office 1, Chisinau MD-2012, Republic of Moldova, Europe
Printed at: see last page
ISBN: 978-620-3-49964-3

Contents

AUTHORS

Jimmy Rolando Molina Rfos, Ph.D. in ICT
Ronal Christopher Elizalde Lopez, Marketing Engineer - Systems Engineer.
Salviano Vicente Nunez Apolo, Ing. Information Technologies.

Introduction

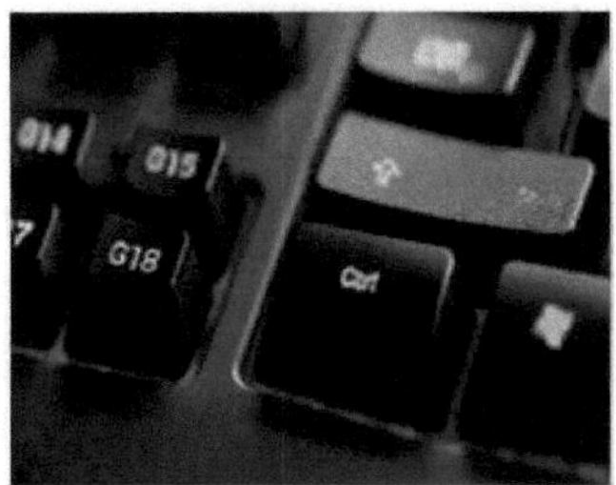

In the development of software, it has always been projected that the system that is being created is on a par with the requirements of the person who asks us for the requirements, therefore the main idea that leads to the resolution of these requirements should not be distorted, for them must follow the standards that have been created to obtain the best possible results, these norms are implemented by the ISO/IEC, in this ISO, the norms of evaluation of quality are established, the same, that throughout this investigation we have taken the norms ISO/IEC 9126, 14598, 25000, these norms or ISO, they are also known as metrics which evaluate the process of development of the software, this process is evaluated in different way according to the norm that we apply, this chosen metric will have sub-processes and rules to follow, for example, if a module is evaluated in any part of the system the obtained data will serve for the modification of the software in case these data do not stick to the main idea of the requirements obtained at the beginning, some metrics also give to know the results of evaluation of each module or part of the software to the person who gave the problem as it is the user or client, in order to minimize the errors that are presented and to be able to change them in time, managing to avoid annoyances at the end, in the delivery of the software, with this aim the metrics of the evaluation of quality have been developed, managing to obtain the best results of the software until the same installation in the machine where it is going to have its useful life as system.

CHAPTER I

ISO/IEC Metrics 9126.

Competences

Defines concepts of ISO metrics
9126
Recognises the characteristics for measuring quality
Identifies the sub-characteristics used in each quality characteristic.
When you have read this unit the **learning outcomes**:

Identify the quality aspects of the ISO 9126 standard.

Identify, classify and describe the main characteristics of the   characteristics of quality evaluation.

Contents

1.1 Quality Model

1.2 External Metrics

1.3 Internal Metrics

1.4 Quality of use metrics

Introduction

ISO 9126 manages to define several quality characteristics, which are quality factors, criteria and metrics. The quality factors allow the specification, i.e. the view of the software from the users' point of view, external view; the criteria, which allow the construction, i.e. the view of the software from the developer's point of view, internal view; and finally the metrics, which allow the control, used to provide the method for performing the evaluation.

1 METRICS ISO/IEC 9126: PRODUCT QUALITY

The ISO 9126 metrics are international standards, which provide the characteristics to be considered for the evaluation of the quality of the software, referring to the user, i.e. the system operator.

Over time, the ISO 9126 metric standard has evolved and now has four main sections on which it is based. These sections stipulate the characteristics that each one defines in order to provide a safe and efficient evaluation of the software. The sections into which this metric is classified are: the quality model, in which 6 characteristics are presented for measurement together with the sub-characteristics they focus on, this is called ISO/IEC 9126-1; the external metrics are the characteristics that allow the general behaviour of the software to be measured in the eyes of the end users within the software environment in which it is established, this is called ISO/IEC 9126-2; the internal metrics are the characteristics of the software to be evaluated, they are static metrics, this is called ISO/IEC 9126-3; and finally the quality in use model, this model generally used for the evaluation of the quality of software development is based fundamentally on 4 important factors which are effectiveness, productivity, security and satisfaction [1], this is called ISO/IEC 9126-4. These metrics were designed for the specification and evaluation of the quality of a given software, including in its evaluation the revision of fundamental and basic characteristics for the correct execution of the software, and the optimal functioning before the final user, to satisfy the needs required by the client.

1.1 Quality Model

In order to evaluate the quality of software in an effective and optimal way, models are established, which are a series of characteristics or phases to be implemented, with which the functionality, the guarantee and the security of the customer's satisfaction with the software can be fully appreciated. The quality model is simply a standard which governs the evaluation of the software.

For this purpose, the software properties are duly characterised, in which six characteristics are fundamental within the ISO/IEC 9126 standard: functionality, reliability, usability, efficiency, maintainability and portability. Each of these characteristics has sub-characteristics for evaluation, verification and quality assurance.

In order to achieve the proper review and specification of the computer system, there are three levels within quality, three levels that help to efficiently evaluate the software, these are the characteristics, features and attributes, which are the entities that are capable of being verified within the software product.

It should be emphasised that the characteristics and sub-characteristics within the system are fixed, i.e. they are already delimited within the standard in order to achieve a correct evaluation. By means of the evaluation or monitoring of these characteristics and sub-characteristics.

The metrics for quality assessment can be person-oriented as well, i.e. it is facilitated by the way people developed the software, the processes they developed, the effectiveness of the tools and the methods used for it. This evaluation is subjective, i.e. it depends on people's perception of the software developed, and can be quantitative or qualitative.

1.1.1 Software Quality

Software quality is based on the mix of evaluation factors within the system that can affect the production of quality software. These factors can be considered as internal or external, what is considered and valued is that the final result satisfies the client and manages to solve the problems for which the project was developed.

Software quality concepts are mainly driven by the ISO standards, which are responsible for assessing both the quality and the product of software.

A definition established by the ISO 8402 standard, mentions that "quality is the set of properties and characteristics of a product or service that make it suitable to satisfy explicit or undefined needs" [2]. [2]

According to the above, it can be mentioned that the quality within the software product is considered as the evaluation of the characteristics or functions that manage to satisfy the purposes or objectives for which the software was developed, thus providing an optimal and efficient result to the client or user.

Several definitions of quality are linked to software engineering, as the metrics evolve, the various concepts of software quality increase and expand. These definitions were varying, having as main idea the same focus as the concepts of the past metrics, so software quality came to be considered as "the degree to which a system, component or process meets the specified requirements and the needs or expectations of the customer or user." [2]

That is to say, quality is taken into account as a category or level, by means of which the system or some product manages to fulfil the objectives set out during the specification of requirements and planning of the project, as well as satisfying the needs required both by the client, who is the one who requested the software, and by the end user(s), who are the ones who will constantly interact with the system, carrying out income, transactions, operations, among others.

It should be emphasised that not only standards or metrics define quality concepts, several authors such as Pressman [3] and Sommerville [4] conceptualise quality within software engineering as "the concordance with established functional and performance requirements, documented development standards and expected characteristics of professionally developed software". [3] Furthermore, they consider software quality assessment as a complex process, which requires following a series of fundamental steps for a correct software development, taking into account the previous conceptualisation, it is mentioned that quality measurement is applicable to any product, in general terms, but, for the realisation within a computer system, it is necessary to consider diverse and complex characteristics in comparison to products outside this field.

1.1.2 Characteristics.

ISO/IEC 9126 within the first model, which is the quality model, has certain characteristics which help to evaluate the software. The characteristics into which this model is divided consist of 6 aspects, within which other sub-characteristics are found. This is due to the fact that the general or main characteristics are very complex to evaluate, i.e. they do not have the necessary indicators or guidelines with which the developers or evaluators can review the quality of the product.

Therefore, by using the sub-characteristics which represent indicators of the evaluation, a complete and optimal quality review of the product can be obtained, because they represent measurable aspects, as well as giving the necessary guidelines for the evaluation procedure.

According to Ruiz, Pena & Castro [5] the characteristics by which software quality is categorised are closely linked to the criterion of usability, and are divided into six, which are as follows:

*   Functionality.
*   Reliability.
*   Usability.
*   Efficiency.
*   Ease of maintenance.
*   Portability.

Each one of them represents a fundamental aspect for the evaluation of the quality of a software product, but at the same time they are very complex to measure, since they are general, that is to say, the way in which each characteristic can be measured is wide. For this, it is necessary to sub-divide each of these characteristics into sub-characteristics, with which the quality evaluation process is simple, fast and above all efficient.

In the following, each characteristic is described together with sub-characteristics for measurement.

1.1.3 Functionality

Functionality encompasses the ability of a product or system to execute functions or properties which satisfy the needs and solve the problems of the customer and user [5]. These functionalities must be established in the planning and scope stipulation of the system, as well as including all these operations internally in the system to be realised.

These functionalities must be able to solve the problems or inconveniences that the user has with the system under specific conditions.

Functionality simply refers to the "ability of the software to provide the services necessary to meet functional requirements" [6]. [6]

That is, it ensures that the software fulfils the stated objective(s), these functionalities provided within the system must supply and cover the needs, requirements, and objectives that were stated within the project proposal, these must be in an impKcite or expKcite way of the users.

This group is composed by attributes or also called characteristics, which allow to qualify the software as a product so that it meets the requirements and satisfies the needs for which it was designed and developed.

In order to achieve a correct and relevant quality assessment, the following sub-characteristics need to be assessed [7]:

- **Adequacy:** This sub-characteristic focuses on the evaluation of the functions and tasks that support the software. It seeks to evaluate whether the functions and operations performed by the system for the management of the corresponding requirements comply with the tasks that were established during planning.

In other words, it assesses whether the operations carried out by the system are the most appropriate and, above all, whether they comply with the tasks to be performed.

- **Accuracy:** This attribute stipulates whether the results of the system executions are in accordance with the needs that the user wishes to satisfy. By means of this attribute, it is possible to evaluate the precision of the product's responses, and whether or not these are the most appropriate for their resolution.

- **Interoperability:** This feature allows to evaluate the interaction of the system with other pre-specified systems. Interoperability means that the system can relate and interact with other systems independently, i.e. systems outside the developed system.

- **Conformity:** This attribute assesses whether the developed product meets the requirements and provides conformity and safety to the customer.

- **Security:** In this point, the security and protection of the data within the system is evaluated, that is, the capacity of the software to protect the information, to keep it safe from unauthorised persons entering, modifying or deleting the information.

Thanks to the above mentioned aspects, it is important to take them into account, as these attributes are measurable in comparison to an assessment of overall system functionality.

1.1.4 Reliability

Reliability is described as the ability of the software product [8] to maintain its performance level correctly, during an established period of time. It establishes whether the program manages to remain stable during its execution, without errors or failures that slow down or crash the system.

This characteristic is also known as reliability, and has a strong relationship with the user and the interaction with the system. The favourable results of this evaluation must be visible and must be able to maintain the correct functioning of the software for the respective requests made by the user for a set period of time and especially under specific conditions.

In order to correctly fulfil the purpose of software reliability assessment, measurable sub-characteristics are established, above all, which allow an optimal evaluation of the developed product. These characteristics or also known as attributes are [5]:

- **Maturity level:** Within this level are the attributes that have a certain relationship with system failures. Maturity can be defined within the Software Engineering environment as the ability to prevent system failures when an error is found.

Examples for a better understanding of software product maturity include warning messages to the user when he/she performs an operation on the software that could generate errors.

In some cases, the maturity level is also considered to "measure the frequency of failure due to software errors" [7]. [7]

• **Fault Tolerance:** This software attribute is closely related to the software's ability to achieve an expected level of performance in situations where software failures may occur.

It is essential to determine and evaluate this attribute, because the system must always maintain performance and operation, no matter what the situation is, but mainly to keep the system stable in case of errors.

Fault tolerance can be defined as "the ability to maintain an expected level of performance in the event of software failures or violations of its expected interface" [7]. [7]

• **Recoverability:** This sub-feature expects and validates that the system succeeds in restoring data that was considered lost or deleted. This usually happens after a failure or alteration that violates the integrity parameters of the classes designed in the applications.

It can be considered as "the ability to re-establish the level of operation and recover data that has been directly affected by a failure, as well as the time and effort required to achieve this" [7]. In other words, the ability of the system to recover from either performance failure or data loss.

• **Reliability compliance:** the latter is only used to verify that the software complies with the attributes related to reliability, i.e. the ability to apply standards, legislation, etc. related to reliability.

The attributes set out above evaluate the software product, to determine whether it ensures good error or failure handling within the software product in any given situation. Several aspects must be considered, including the consideration and prevention of errors through the design of the system, and the correct handling of these errors, i.e. how to handle errors in case they occur.

1.1.5 Usability

Usability is the ability of the software to be understood, learned and above all the ease of use it possesses.

Within it, the criteria of functionality, reliability and efficiency interfere and are used to achieve a correct evaluation of the quality of the software product.

The usability of the application must be compatible with the acquisition of new knowledge procedures to achieve a correct execution of the application [9]. Usability inspections consist of a series of analysis and data collection methods. The main objective is to analyse the different aspects of the application in order to incorporate the most appropriate user interface designs.

Usability can only be evaluated through the interaction of the users and the system, i.e. it is an evaluation that focuses on the end-user, indicating how easy it is for the user to manipulate the software, how easy it is for the user to understand the processes, the interface and the results it generates.

According to Ruiz, Pena & Castro, usability is "the ability of a software product to be understandable, learnable, usable and attractive to the user when it is used under specific conditions" [5]. [5]

As quality evaluation standards evolve, the characteristics involved in product evaluation include ease of use of the product, ease of learning the product, ease of doing a certain task, ease of installing the product, ease of finding information in the manual, ease of understanding the information, and finally the usability of the help examples.

Usability characterisation measures the degree to which the system is optimal for use and management by end users, and can be considered as the "set of attributes that relate to the effort required for use and the individual evaluation of that use by an established or impKicit set of users" [1]. [1]

Like the previous characteristics, usability has sub-characteristics which are directed towards the user:

• **Ease of understanding:** This attribute refers to the effort required by the end user to recognise the logical structure of the software. Within it, guidelines are established to achieve an easy understanding of how the system works, and how it is used for the tasks and certain conditions that the application presents, as well as the documentation and the help guides that are generated with the programme. In other words, ease of understanding indicates how easy it is for the user to learn the functionalities and operations of the system, including the logical concepts and their applications.

• **Ease of learning:** Within this attribute, fields are established to evaluate the product in accordance with its capacity to be understood by users. In the ease of learning, it is essential to take into account that the systems must be intuitive both in their operation and in their interface, so that the user does not have greater complexity when trying to manage any operation within the system.

• **Operability:** Or also known as operability, and is defined as the way in which the software allows the user to operate and manipulate it. It is essential that the software is easy to manipulate, so that the user is able to perform the operations he/she needs to perform quickly, easily and efficiently.

To measure the usability of a system, three main attributes are established [10]:

• **Effectiveness**: This is defined as the precision and accuracy of the application for the user to achieve the objectives specified in the application. This includes the ease of understanding and learning by the user.

• **Efficiency**: Efficiency is defined as the resources employed to achieve specified objectives with accuracy and completeness.

• **Satisfaction**: The comfort provided by the application to the end user is evaluated, considering the acceptance of the application by the users.

1.1.6 Efficiency

This characteristic allows the evaluation of the software based on its performance and the amount of resources used during its development process. Efficiency is defined as the ability of a software product to achieve appropriate software performance, which is fundamentally related to the amount of resources that are employed to create the system, under given conditions.

Efficiency in general terms can be defined as the ability, capacity or property that is possessed to obtain an optimal and favourable result, comparing the functionality of the same and the resources that are used during its execution.

This is a fundamental attribute in the evaluation of the software product, both for better performance and for optimal development. What is sought through efficiency is to develop software that directly performs the operations for which it was designed, and that the least amount of resources are used during the development process.

"The efficiency of the software is the form of adequate performance, according to the number of resources used under the given conditions. It must take into account other aspects such as hardware configuration, operating system, among others." [8]

It can be determined as the degree to which the software performs its functions optimally, and makes optimal and expected use of system resources.

Similarly, characteristics are established to measure the efficiency of a software product, since it is not possible to evaluate it in a general way, these are:

• **Time of use:** This attribute establishes the behaviour with respect to the time taken to perform an operation in spertfico. "Software attributes related to response times and data processing times" [7]. [7] This sub-characteristic is important because it stipulates the response times of the developed system, and also analyses and evaluates the data processing required by the operations carried out within the product, evaluating the efficiency and whether the response time of the operations carried out is correct and efficient.

A clear example of time-of-use evaluation is the determination of the response time of the system to a functionality requested by the end user, in addition to analysing the amount of code used to perform the desired process.

• **Resources used:** this feature focuses on the

behaviour with respect to the resources used during the software development process. "Attributes of the software relating to the amount of resources used and the duration of their use in the performance of its functions. [7] This sub-characteristic is important because it provides more control and assurance over the development process, and how the system will perform under the requested conditions. In this part, not only the amount of resources that have been used is evaluated, but also the duration that these resources will have within the project, at the moment of realising some main function of the system.

Efficiency compliance can also be considered as one of its attributes or characteristics.

• **Efficiency compliance:** This attribute represents the software's ability to comply with standards and norms that are related to efficiency in general. In this point, it is evaluated that the software products correctly comply with all the requirements that the systems have based on the effectiveness that the systems provide by using the resources in an optimal way and quickly fulfilling the functions that the system must fulfil.

1.1.7 Ease of Maintenance

This characteristic refers to the attributes that allow to measure the effort that is necessary to develop and thus make modifications to the system, either due to bug fixes or sometimes due to increased system requirements.

"Maintainability is the ability of software to be modified. Including corrections or enhancements to the software, to changes in the environment, and to functional requirements specifications." [8]

This point is used to represent modifications or the ease with which the software can be modified. There are several factors that affect the use or evaluation of the software, and that require certain modifications to the software. Among these, once the software has been made, it must be corrected, because it presents errors during the execution process, this can be, for example, a failure in the validation of the fields, a failure for the communication with the database, or that the internal calculations made are not the adequate ones.

Another circumstance in which a software must be modified is when there is a modification in the requirements, this can be to add some requirement or simply to improve, modify, or eliminate some field or requirement of the system. This is provided when the client decides to implement new functionalities to the system or simply wishes to perform some other action, such as modifying it, eliminating it or in certain cases improving it.

Finally, another circumstance that arises is the improvement of the software, which tends to occur mainly in mobile and web applications. This case occurs when you want to create a system update, a new version or implement some new functionality to it. Examples of these cases are presented in mobile applications, which must be constantly improving, increasing its functions to get the customer's attention.

Ease of maintenance is essential because it allows improvements and modifications to be made to the system without the need to create the system from scratch. A clean and understandable structure and coding are the main points that allow to increase an operation to an already existing system, otherwise several problems would be generated including, the delay in the time of development, and the confusion and appearance of possible errors.

The changes you wish to make can be of a small magnitude or of a large magnitude, this will depend on what you wish to modify. At this point it is possible to modify from the user interface, the location of buttons, the design of the same, or simply because they are not attractive to the client; it is also possible to modify the structural or functional part of the system, that is to say to make a change in the processes that it carries out.

It presents the following sub-characteristics to achieve a perfect maintainability assessment within the software product.

• **Analysis capability:** "Relating to the effort required to diagnose deficiencies or causes of failures, or to identify the parts that need to be modified. [7] This sub-characteristic specifies the way in which the software can be diagnosed for deficiencies or causes of failures, in this point stages and processes such as coding, design and documentation of changes are considered.

This point is fundamental, because it evaluates and determines the aspects of the software for a diagnosis of the possible deficiencies that it may have, or simply the causes of possible failures that the system may present.

In addition, the stages, parts or processes that can be modified within the system are analysed, as well as the contingencies that may arise.

• **Modifiability:** "Measures the effort required to modify aspects of the software, remove bugs or adapt the software to work in a different environment". [7]

Also known as changeability, this indicates the ability of the software product to achieve a future modification, which must be specified and then implemented.

It must be analysed so that the programmer or the person making the changes can make them quickly, simply and optimally.

•   **Stability:** "Allows to assess the risks of unexpected effects due to modifications made to the software" [7]. [7]

This attribute represents the risk relations that can present the effects of unexpected modifications. This point is fundamental because it allows the system execution process to be kept stable, as well as representing the way in which the software is prepared for the modifications of the changes required by the client or by the development environment.

•   **Testability:** "Refers to the effort required to validate the software once it has been modified". [7] This attribute specifies the manner in which the software allows for testing and evaluation of the modifications that have been made. This action must be done on the condition that it does not put data or information at risk, or even worse, put the developed system at risk.

The tests performed are important because they make it possible to verify whether the tests carried out within the system are easy and whether the modifications made do not alter the structure of the project.

1.1.8 Portability

This characteristic refers to the ability of the software to be transferred or transported from one environment to another. Within this characteristic is the facility to implement functions or simply the system in general from one development environment to another, without the need to make any modification to the software. Furthermore, when transferring from one environment to another, no data is lost and no errors are created.

The most common problem in software development is the difficulty of being transported to another environment, which can be evaluated at two points: being transported from one development environment to another, or being transported from one installation site to another.

In the first case, it must be verified that the coding, implementation and design do not interfere or are dependent on the environment in which it is being developed, i.e. when the system is moved from one environment to another, it does not generate errors or failures either by the code or by the resources that were previously used.

In the second case, the transfer from one place of execution to another is specified, i.e. that the application or system can be installed on another computer without any problem, and above all that it can be installed without generating errors.

Among the features found in the portability are:

•   **Adaptability:** Adaptability refers to the evaluation of the adaptability of the software in different environments, without the need for modifications to make it run smoothly. Adaptability is one of the main requirements of the system, because software that can be installed anywhere, without changing its performance, is more efficient and effective than other systems. During the creation of the system, care should be taken that no dependencies are made on the main features of a single computer, or a single user.

•   **Ease of installation:** this characteristic represents the effort required to install the software in a given environment. This point specifies the diversity to achieve a correct installation of the system, i.e. that the system can be installed in different order and for different users, without the need to make modifications to the system or code to ensure that the operation of the system does not change.

- **Conformance:** "Allows to evaluate whether the software adheres to standards or conventions related to portability". [7] This point evaluates whether the software complies with the corresponding requirements and qualities for good portability.
- **Replaceability:** "The ability of software to be replaced by other software of the same type, and for the same purpose". [8] Replaceability, or also known as substitutability, specifies the ability of the software to succeed in implementing a replacement of that software with improved software designed for the same type of system and for the same intended purpose.

An example of this characteristic can be considered, when replacing a new application, in cases generally of web or mobile applications, new versions of the same are created, in which improvements are simply made to the programme, without the need to modify data, or radically change the internal structure. The system must have the possibility and ability to be modified or upgraded, simply by running the new application and migrating the data to the new software, which may be from a different vendor or from the same vendor.

1.2 External Metrics.

The external quality metrics is the degree to which the product manages to satisfy the explicit needs of the software under specific conditions, at this point the purpose is evaluated and up to what point the product manages to satisfy the needs, it is measured and evaluated under dynamic properties, considered as dynamic metrics, it is carried out in the quality control stages of the software life cycle.

1.3 Internal Metrics.

The internal metrics of a software product are defined as the attributes of a product or system that determine the ability to satisfy the problems and needs presented by the user in an expKcite and impKcite manner under specified conditions.

It can be measured and evaluated by characteristics of the system requirement documents. This evaluation is performed in early stages of the software life cycle, in which it is possible to measure, control and evaluate the internal quality of the software product.

1.4 Quality of use metrics.

"Quality in use is the quality of the software that the end-user reflects, the way in which the end-user manages to perform the processes with satisfaction, efficiency and accuracy.

Quality in use must ensure the testing or review of all the options that the user works with on a daily basis and the processes that he/she performs sporadically related to the same software". [8]

1.4.1 Characteristics

- **Safety**: "is the ability of the software to comply with the permitted risk levels for both potential physical damage and potential data risks". [8]
- **Satisfaction**: The ability of the software to satisfy the needs of the client and end user, in addition to meeting the requirements and objectives established in the planning stage.
- **Productivity**: "ability of the software to allow users to expend the appropriate

amount of resources in relation to the Efficiency (Effectiveness) obtained". [8]

• **Efficiency**: The ability of the software to provide the user with accurate results using the least amount of resources possible, and obtaining the best result.

| IMPORTANT CONCEPTS

• **Portability:** The ability of a system to move from one location or environment to another. It has certain characteristics that must be taken into account such as adaptability, ease of installation, compliance and ease of replacement.

• **Maintainability:** It is the capacity of a system to be modified, this aspect takes into account the possible modifications due to improvements (creation of versions), or due to a change of requirements in the software functionalities, by the client.

• **Functionality:** It is the capacity of a product to fulfil the functions and operations for which it was designed. It must be able to solve the needs presented by the client when using the system. This has characteristics such as adequacy, accuracy, interoperability, compliance, and security.

• **Recoverability:** The ability of the system to recover data and information that has been lost after the action of a failure. It is able to re-establish the execution level and recover the desired data.

- **Maturity:** It is the ability of the system to tolerate or measure the frequency of failures that may exist due to errors in the software. It evaluates the ability to prevent system failures that are generated when an error is found.

FURTHER READING

From the academic article: "Software Quality Assessment Model Based on Fuzzy Logic, Applied to Usability Metrics according to ISO/IEC 9126", by Hugo F. Arboleda Jimenez. MSc.Gustavo Alberto Ruiz, Alejandro Pena, and Carlos Arturo Castro, which is available at the following link:

http://www.redalyc. org/htm l/1331/133114988005/

Develop the following questions:

1. How does the IEE standard describe software quality?
2. What is a fundamental aspect of software quality? ^Why?
3. What are the main characteristics of software quality?
4. What are the subjective measures that can be used for quality analysis?
5. Define the maintenance friendliness characteristic and specify its sub-characteristics.

From the article "Usability in Mobile Applications", by Enriquez Juan Gabriel, and Casas Sandra Isabel. Available at the following link:

https://dialnet.unirioja.es/descarga/articulo/5123524.pdf

Develop the following questions:

1. What are the attributes considered to measure the degree of usability of a software application?
2. What are the characteristics that a metric must fulfil?

3. Define the usability metric ISO 9241-11.
4. Can the attributes of an application be directly measured? Why?
5. What is the classification of metrics and define each of them?

WORKSHOP N° 1

Fill in the following table of the characteristics of the model of the ISO/IEC 9126 quality standard with its respective sub-characteristics.

QUALITY MODEL	
Features	**Sub-characteristics**
Functionality	- - - -
Reliability	- - -
Usability	- - -
Efficiency	- -
Maintainability	- - - -
Portability	- - -

Mention a real life situation, which exemplifies the following sub-characteristics mentioned.

Feature: Efficiency.

Sub-feature: Time of use.

Example:

Characteristics: Ease of maintenance.

Sub-characteristic: Modification capability.

Example:

Feature: Portability.

Sub-characteristic: Adaptability.

Example:

WORKSHOP N° 3 -

Relate each of the concepts with the characteristics that corresponds.

The system is able to restore the data that was considered lost or deleted.	**Replacement capacity**
the evaluation of the software's	**Fault Tolerance**

adaptability in different environments, without the need for modification	
Ability to achieve a specific level of performance in situations where software failures may occur.	**Adaptability**
The ability of the software to be replaced by other software of the same type, and for the same purpose.	**Recoverability**
Ability to prevent system failures when errors are encountered.	**Maturity level**

EVALUATION

1	FORMAT	SIMPLE	
	Context		
	Approach	**When we talk about fault tolerance for software quality we are referring to...?**	
	OPTION A	The ability of the system to recover from either performance failures or loss of information.	
	OPTION B	The ability of the software to be understood by the user.	
	OPTION C	The ability of the software to protect the information from external agents.	
	OPTION D	The ability of the software to achieve a specific level of performance in situations where failures may occur.	
	Correct Answer	D	
	Level	1	
	Operation Cognitive	Application of Concepts and Principles	
2	FORMAT	SIMPLE	
	Context		
	Approach	**^Which sub-characteristics belong to the functionality?**	
	OPTION A	Maturity level, Fault tolerance, Recoverability.	
	OPTION B	Adequacy, Accuracy, Interoperability.	
	OPTION C	Time of use, Resources used.	
	OPTION D	Ease of understanding, Ease of learning, Ease of operation.	
	Correct Answer	B	
	Level	1	
	Cognitive Operation	Application of Concepts and Principles	
3	FORMAT	SIMPLE	
	Context		
	Approach	**The satisfaction quality of use metric refers to...?**	
	OPTION A	Capability of the software to meet risk levels for potential physical and data damage.	

	OPTION B	Ability of the software to meet end-user expectations.
	OPTION C	Ability of the software to allow the appropriate amount of resources to be expended.
	OPTION D	Software capability to facilitate the achievement of objectives with precision.
	Correct Answer	B
	Level	1
	Cognitive Operation	Application of Concepts and Principles
	FORMAT	SIMPLE
	Context	
	Approach	**The Effectiveness quality of use metric refers to...?**
	OPTION A	Capability of the software to meet risk levels for potential physical and data damage.
	OPTION B	Ability of the software to meet end-user expectations.
	OPTION C	Ability of the software to allow the appropriate amount of resources to be expended.
	OPTION D	Software capability to facilitate the achievement of objectives with precision.
	Correct Answer	D
	Level	1
4	**Cognitive Operation**	Application of Concepts and Principles
	FORMAT	SIMPLE
	Context	
	Approach	**When we talk about maturity level in software quality we refer to...?**
	OPTION A	The ability of the system to recover from either performance failure or data loss.
	OPTION B	The software's ability to prevent system failures when errors are encountered.
	OPTION C	The ability of the software to protect information from external agents.
	OPTION D	The ability of the software to achieve an expected level of performance in situations where failures may occur.
	Correct Answer	B
	Level	1
5	**Cognitive Operation**	Application of Concepts and Principles
6	**FORMAT**	**SIMPLE**
	Context	
	Approach	**What does the following concept refer to?** *These are the characteristics of the software to be evaluated, they are static metrics.*

	OPTION A	Internal Metrics
	OPTION B	External Metrics
	OPTION C	Quality Model
	OPTION D	Quality of use model.
	Correct Answer	A
	Level	1
	Operation Cognitive	Application of Concepts and Principles
7	FORMAT	SIMPLE
	Context	
	Approach	**Is the quality model composed of external and internal metrics?**
	OPTION A	True
	OPTION B	False
	Correct Answer	A
	Level	1
	Cognitive Operation	Application of Concepts and Principles
8	FORMAT	SIMPLE
	Context	
	Approach	**^Maintainability feature refers to...?**
	OPTION A	Attributes that allow to measure the effort that is necessary to develop and thus make modifications to the system.
	OPTION B	The software's ability to prevent system failures when errors are encountered.
	OPTION C	The ability of the software to protect the information from external agents.
	OPTION D	The ability of the software to achieve a specific level of performance in situations where failures may occur.
	Correct Answer	A
	Level	1
	Cognitive Operation	Application of Concepts and Principles
9	FORMAT	SIMPLE
	Context	
	Approach	**What is the definition of software quality?**
	OPTION A	A evaluation of the different features or functions that satisfy the purposes for which the software was designed.
	OPTION B	Simple process, which requires the specification of a series of fundamental steps for a correct development of the software
	OPTION C	Process of specifying and evaluating the quality of a given piece of software
	OPTION D	are international standards, which provide the characteristics to be considered in order to achieve software quality assessment.

	Correct Answer	A
	Level	1
	Operation Cognitive	Application of Concepts and Principles
	FORMAT	SIMPLE
	Context	
	Approach	**Is software quality based on the evaluation of only external factors of the system?**
	OPTION A	True
	OPTION B	False
	Correct Answer	B
	Level	
10	Operation Cognitive	Application of Concepts and Principles

GLOSSARY (Alphabetical order)

- **Accessibility**: "Considerations taken into account by possible physical, visual, auditory or other limitations of users". [11]

• **Quality:** "the degree to which the software possesses a desired combination of attributes, this combination of attributes shall be clearly specified". [11]

• **Errors**: "The errors that the user makes when using the application and the severity of these errors". [11]

• **Portability:** "Ability of the application to be transferred from one environment to another (different platforms)". [11]

• **Security**: "Ability to achieve acceptable levels of risk. Availability of mechanisms that control and protect the application and stored data" [11].

| SOLUTION (EVALUATION)

1. D) The ability of the software to achieve a specified level of performance in potentially faulty situations.
2. B) Adequacy, Accuracy, Interoperability.
3. B) Ability of the software to meet end-user expectations.
4. D) Software capability to facilitate the achievement of objectives with precision.
5. B) The software's ability to prevent system failures when errors are encountered.
6. A) Internal Metrics
7. A) True
8. A) Attributes that allow to measure the effort that is necessary to develop and thus make modifications to the system.
9. A) An evaluation of the different features or functions that satisfy the purposes for which the software was designed.
10. B) false

CHAPTER II

Metrica 25000.

Competences

Identify the basic characteristics of Metric 25000 within the scope of Software Engineering.

Know the parameters that Metrics offer as a guide for an excellent software project.

Use of metrics in Software Engineering projects.

The **learning outcomes** will be achieved by the end of this unit:

itify the characteristics of the Rich 25000 that are used in the different software projects.

You identify the processes that occur and the effect of the application of metrics.

Contents

2.1 Structure of the Standard.

2.2 Division of the Quality Model

2 ISO /IEC 25000

ISO/IEC 25000, known as AQuaRe (System and Software Quality Requirements and Evaluation), aims to provide a single framework for the software quality evaluation process.

"ISO/IEC 25000 is the result of the evolution and implementation of earlier standards, notably ISO/IEC 9126, which describes the specifics of a software product quality model, and ISO/IEC 14598, which addressed the software product evaluation process. "Invalid specified source.

Division of ISO/IEC 25000.

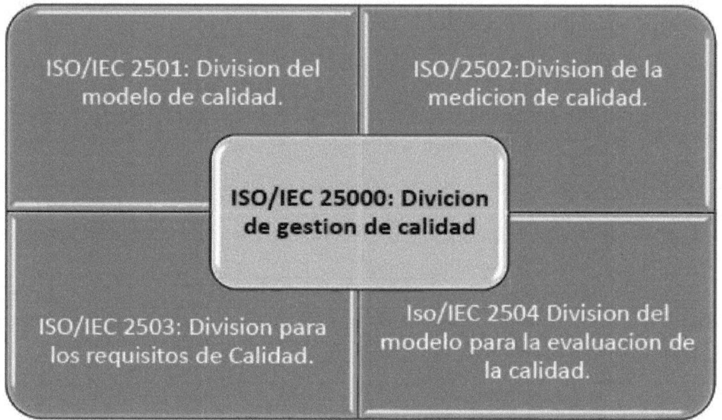

Source:https://iso25000.com/index.php/normasiso25000?limit=4&start=4

2.1 Structure of the ISO/IEC 25000 standard

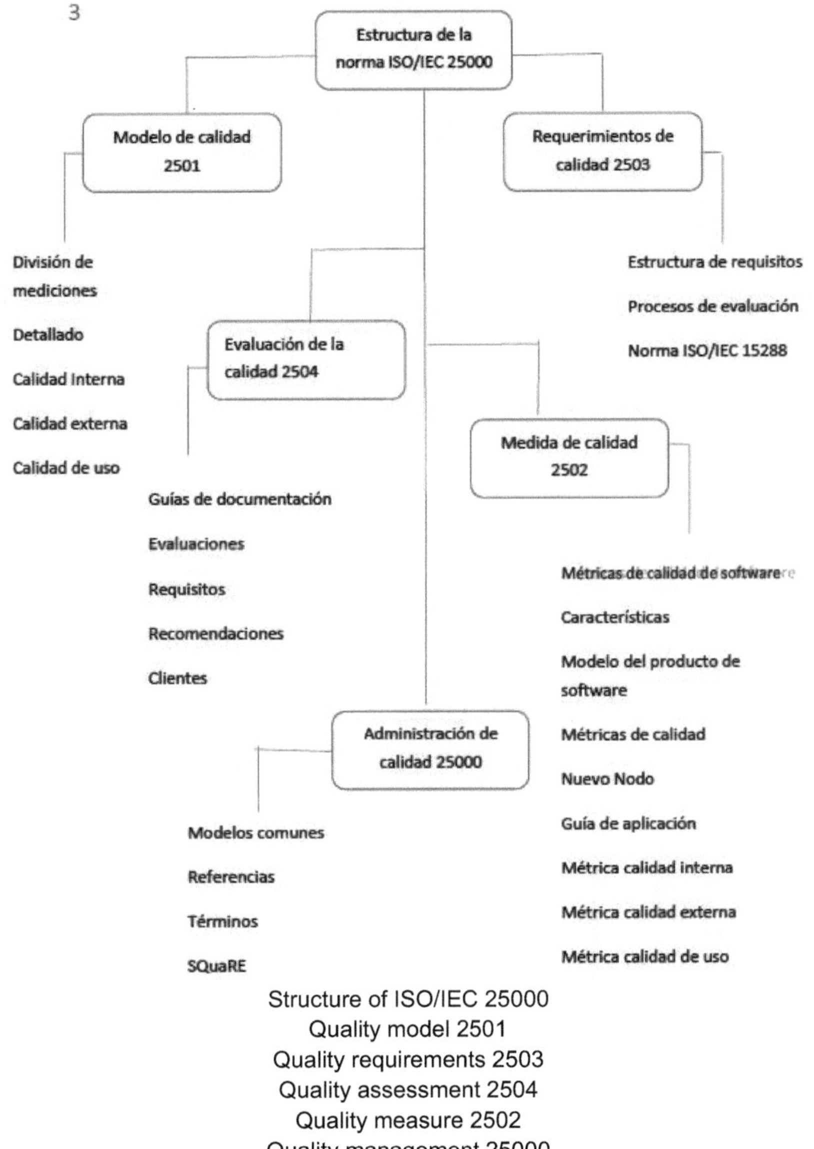

Structure of ISO/IEC 25000
Quality model 2501
Quality requirements 2503
Quality assessment 2504
Quality measure 2502
Quality management 25000
Measurement Division Detailed Internal Quality External Quality Quality Quality of Use
A
Documentation Guides Evaluations Assessments Requirements Recommendations Clients

Software quality metrics Characteristics Software product model Quality metrics New Node Application guide Internal quality metric External quality metric Quality of use metric
Common models References SQuaRE terms
Requirements structure Assessment processes ISO/IEC 15288 standard

3.1 ISO/IEC 25000 Division of the quality model

The quality division includes internal and external characteristics for quality.
of use of a software. It is currently made up of:

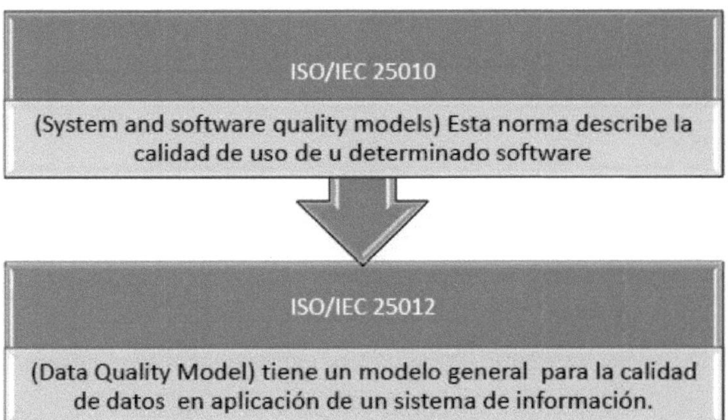

ISO/IEC 25010
(System and software quality models) This standard describes the quality of use of a given software product.
ISO/IEC 25012
(Data Quality Model) has a general model for data quality in an information system application.

3.2 ISO/IEC 2502 division of quality measurement.

These standards refer to a quality measurement of the product, they are composed of:

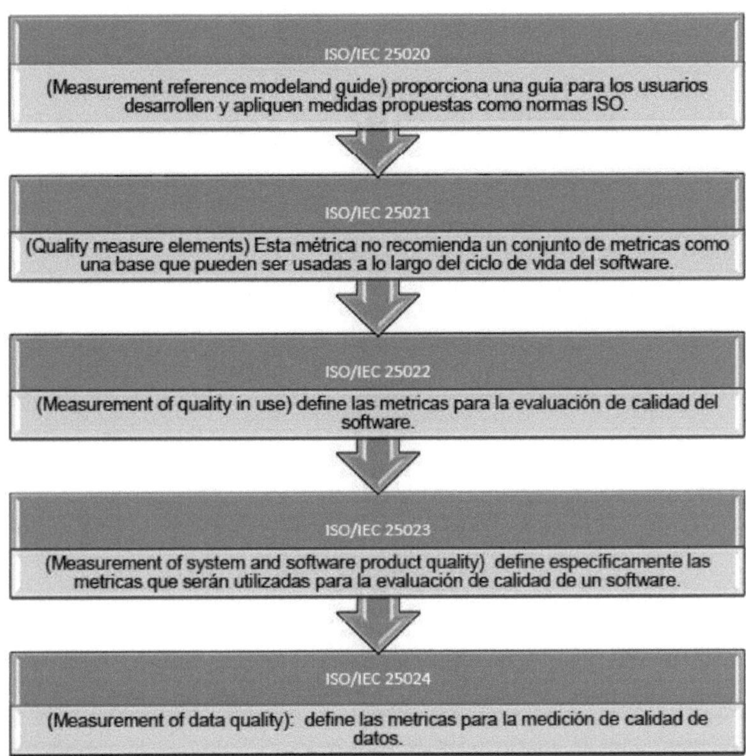

ISO/IEC 25020

(Measurement reference model and guide) provides guidance for users to develop and apply proposed measures as ISO standards.

ISO/IEC 25021

(Quality measure elements) This metric does not recommend a set of metrics as a basis that can be used throughout the software lifecycle.

ISO/IEC 25022

(Measurement of quality in use) defines the metrics for software quality assessment.

ISO/IEC 25023

(Measurement of system and software product quality) specifically defines the metrics to be used for software quality assessment.

ISO/IEC 25024

(Measurement of data quality: defines the metrics for the measurement of data quality.

ISO/IEC 2503: Division for Quality Requirements.

This standard is in charge of specifying the quality requirements that can be used in a software

can be used in a software project that we are developing,

is composed of:

ISO/IEC 2504 Division of the quality assessment model.

This standard provides requirements and recommendations necessary to carry out the software product evaluation process, and consists of the following standards.

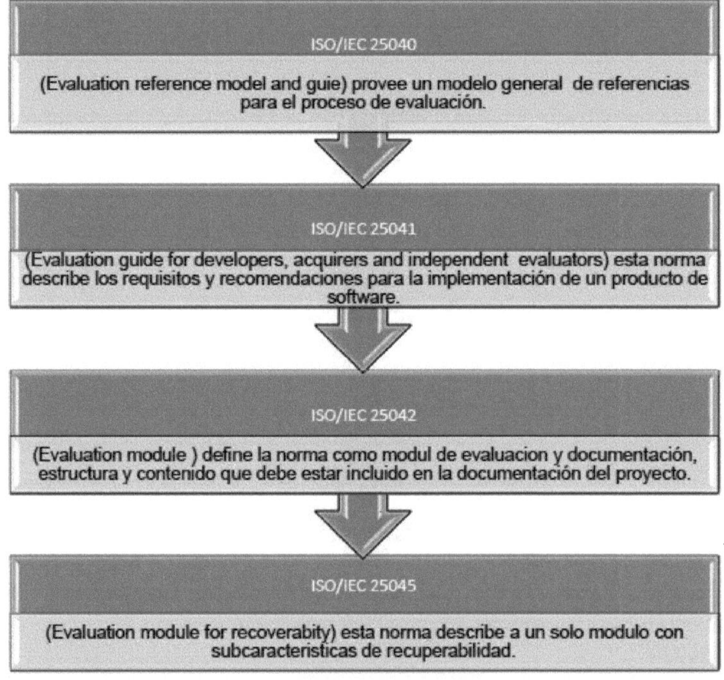

ISO/IEC 25040

(Evaluation reference model and guie) provides a general reference model for the evaluation process.

ISO/IEC 25041

(Evaluation guide for developers, acquirers and independent evaluators) this standard describes the requirements and recommendations for the implementation of a software product.

ISO/IEC 25042

(Evaluation module) defines the standard as evaluation module and documentation, structure and content to be included in the project documentation.

ISO/IEC 25045

(Evaluation module for recoverability) this standard describes a single module with recoverability sub-characteristics.

Processes for carrying out the evaluation
The ISO/IEC 25000 metric defines the assessment process in 5 processes which are as follows:

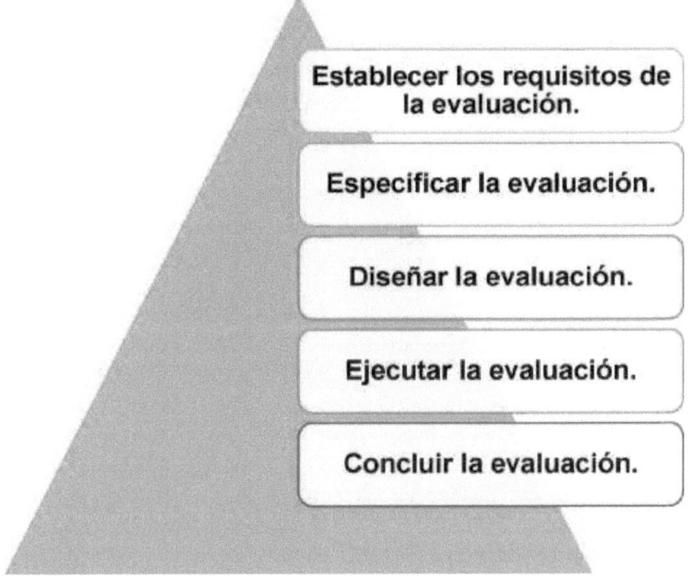

Establish the purpose of the evaluation
"This task documents the purpose for which the organisation wants to assess the quality of its software product (to ensure the quality of the product, to decide whether to accept a product, to determine the feasibility of the project under development, to compare the quality of the product with competing products, etc.)." Source specified not valid.
The purpose of the assessment is to document the purpose for which the software quality assessment is required in order to determine the (product quality) and ensure the development of the software.
Obtain product quality requirements.
"This task identifies the stakeholders of the software product (developers, potential purchasers, users, suppliers, etc.) and specifies the quality requirements of the product using a certain quality model." Source specified not validated.
In order to obtain the product quality requirements, we proceed to identify and specify the quality requirements according to the metrics we use, generally these requirements are established by the users and developers in charge of the software.
Identify the parts of the product to be assessed
"The parts of the software product included in the evaluation must be identified and documented. The type of product to be evaluated (requirements specification, design diagrams, test documentation, etc.) depends on the phase in the lifecycle in which the evaluation is performed and the purpose of the evaluation. "Source specified not valid....

In the process of product identification it is very important to document the parts of the evaluation and the corrections that are generated in the course of the software development, as well as the possible failed tests that are generated.

Define the rigour of the evaluation

"The rigour of the assessment should be defined in terms of the purpose and intended use of the software product, for example based on aspects such as security risk, economic risk or environmental risk. Depending on the rigour, it can be established which techniques are applied and what results are expected from the evaluation. "Source specified not valid....

In the process of defining the rigour of the assessment is the evaluation of possible safety, economic or environmental risks, on the basis of which the expected results of the assessment are implemented.

ISO standard for the quality of a software product

"In 1991 the ISO (International Organization for Standardization) published its quality model for software product evaluation (ISO 9126:1991), which was extended with revisions until 2004, giving rise to the current standard ISO/IEC 9126 "Software Engineering. Product Quality". ISO/IEC 9126 proposes a set of characteristics, sub-characteristics and attributes to break down the quality of a software product. It proposes six properties (functionality, reliability, usability, efficiency, maintainability and portability)" which are divided into subcategories, which will be detailed below **"Invalid specified source...".**

Creation of the Quality Standard ISO/IEC 25000

This standard was born out of the inconsistencies between ISO9126 and ISO14598 in 2005.

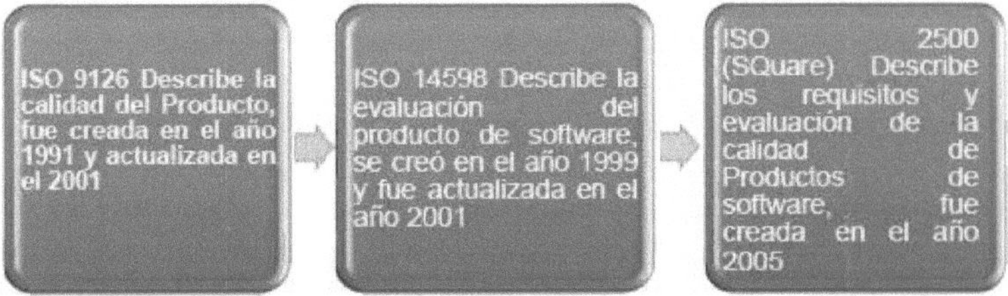

Differences between ISO 9126 and ISO 25000

Here are the main differences between these two quality metrics.

ISO/IEC 9126	ISO/IEC 25000
4- Functionality	4- Functional Adequacy
4- Reliability	4- Security
4- Usability	4- Compatibility
4- Efficiency	4- Reliability
4- Maintainability	4- Usability
4- Portability	4- Performance efficiency
	4- Marketability
	4- Portability

The ISO/IEC 25000 Metric defines a software product quality lifecycle and is divided into three phases:
4- The product development phase defines the internal quality.
4- The product testing phase defines the external quality.
4- The product development phase defines the quality of use.

Structure of Internal Metrics.	Structure of External Metrics.
- Applies to a non-executable software product. - Application during the stages of its development. - They allow the quality of intermediate deliverables to be measured. - They allow the quality of the final product to be predicted. - They allow the user to initiate corrective actions early in the development cycle.	- They apply to an executable software product. - They allow the quality of the final product to be measured.

Metrics of Functionality.

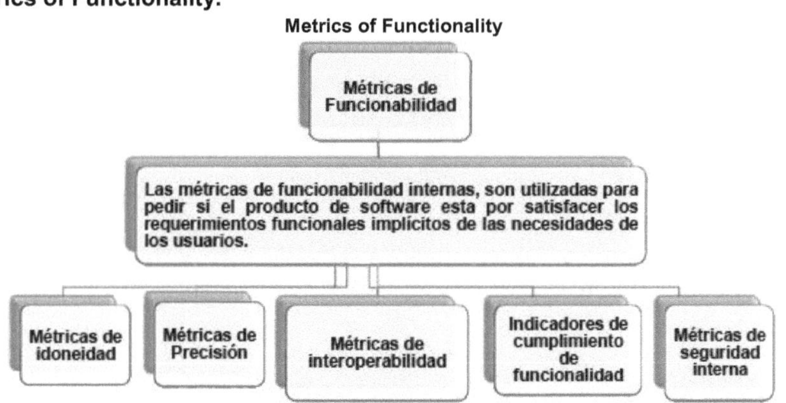

Internal functionality metrics are used to ask whether the software product is about to satisfy the implicit functional requirements of the users' needs.
Adequacy Metrics Accuracy Metrics Interoperability Metrics
Functionality compliance indicators
Internal security metrics

Reliability Metrics.

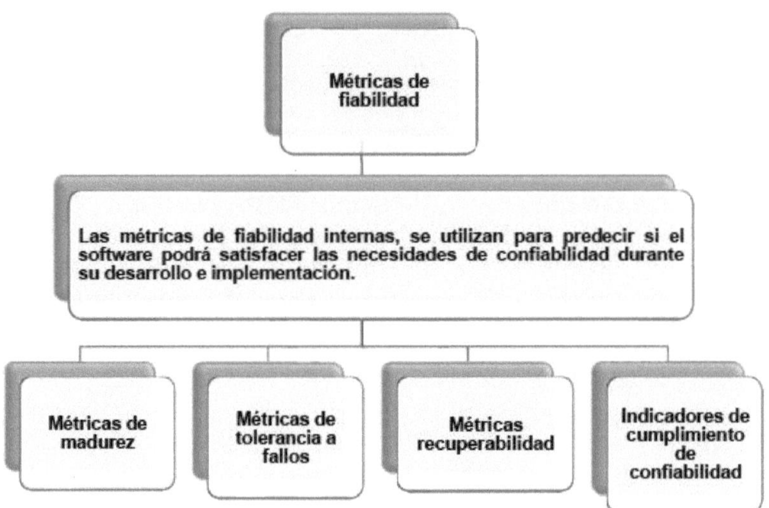

Reliability metrics
Internal reliability metrics are used to predict whether the software will be able to meet reliability needs during development and deployment.
Maturity metrics
Fault tolerance metrics
Recoverability metrics
Reliability compliance indicators

Efficiency Metrics

Efficiency Metrics

These metrics are used to predict the efficiency of the behaviour of the software product during the respective test run.

Behavioural metrics time

Resource utilisation metrics

Efficiency compliance indicators

Changes in maintainability characteristics between ISO 25000 and ISO 25010
"For ISO 25010, the sub-characteristics that make up maintainability are: analysability, modifiability, testability and reusability. There are two new sub-characteristics: reusability and modifiability.

The modifiability sub-characteristic combines two sub-characteristics of ISO 9126: changeability and stability. And standard compliance, which is a sub-characteristic in ISO 9126, is now outside the scope of the quality model in ISO 25010 "Source specified not valid".

ISO 25010 is composed of two sub-characteristics, the modifiability characteristic combines ISO 9126 due to compliance with these standards and the ISO 9126 sub-characteristic which is out of scope of the quality model in ISO/IEC 25010.

Benefits Metrica ISO/IEC 25000

4- It represents the quality of the software.

4- Statement of needs or expectations in terms of external quality and internal quality.

4- Allows for greater efficiency in the definition of the software.

4- Proposes the evaluation of intermediate products.

4- Improves the quality of the product.

Benefits of ISO/IEC 25000 for the organisation.

• "Aligns the objectives of the software with the real needs demanded of it. "**Source specified not valid.**

• "Avoiding inefficiencies and maximising the profitability and quality of the software product. On the other hand, certifying software increases customer satisfaction and improves the company's image. "**Source specified not valid.**

• "Meet contractual requirements and demonstrate to customers that software quality is paramount. "**Source specified not valid.**

• "The process of periodic evaluations helps to continuously monitor performance and improvement. "**Source specified not valid.**

Analytical Analysis:

One of the advantages of this standard is that it is based on others that have already been tested and proved to be efficient in the production of a system for an organisation. Applying standards such as ISO/IEC 25000 is of vital importance as it provides proof of the efficiency of many of the characteristics that software must fulfil in order to be productive.

*   "By demonstrating the organisation's commitment to software quality. "**Source specified not valid.**
Analytical Analysis:
For the client to find a product that meets all the requirements for which it was requested is a source of great satisfaction, therefore this standard guarantees the client that the organisation assumes responsibility for the work to be carried out, however small the project.

| IMPORTANT CONCEPTS

*   **ISO/IEC 2500 Metric:** Establishes the quality of the software product and is composed of quality characteristics, which are composed of sub-characteristics, thus establishing the quality measures of the software product.
*   **Efficiency Metric:** this metric allows to measure the behaviour and the functionality of the system itself.
*   **Usability Metric:** It allows to measure when the software can be understood, learnt, operated and attracted.
*   **Quality Requirements Division:** these requirements help to specify quality and can be used in the quality requirements of the software product being implemented.
*   **Selection of evaluation modules:** in this task, quality metrics, techniques and tools are selected. These metrics allow reliable comparisons with decision making criteria.
*   **Division of quality management:** in ISO/IEC 25000 it is divided into the following metrics.
4-   ISO/IEC 25010
5-   ISO/IEC 25012

FURTHER READING

Metrica ISO/IEC 25000 Software Development Guide available on the page
web: https://www.ecured.cu/ISO/IEC 25000
Develop the following questions:
1.   What is the benefit of using the Evaluation metric?
2.   For what purpose were the quality metrics implemented?
3.   Why are quality metrics important?
4.   What is the structure of the ISO/IEC 25000 quality metrics?
5.   In which year is the first quality metric implemented?
From the analysed article (Clasificacion y evaluación de metricas de Mantebilidad Aplicables a Productos de Software Libre) written by "Jose M. Ruiz, Cristhian D. Pacifico, Martin M. Perez" available in the following link.
http://sedici.unlp.edu.ar/bitstream/handle/10915/61928/Documento complete.p df-PDFA.pdf?sequence=1
Develop the following questions:
1.   What is the function of quality metrics?
2.   What are the benefits of applying it in software development?
3.   What is the main advantage of using ISO/IEC 25000 metrics?
From the article (La norma ISO/IEC 2500 y el proyecto KEMIS para automatizacion

con software libre), written by "Jose Marcos, Alicia Arroyo, Javier Garzas, Mario Piattini", available on the website.
http://www.redalyc.org/pdf/922/92218339013.pdf

Develop the following questions:
1. Specify the ISO standard for the quality of a software product?
2. What are the product metrics and their measurement with open source software?
3. Define the quality of the quality metrics?
4. Specify the quality attributes?
5. Specify the quality metric 2503.

WORKSHOP N° 1

Write down the process for carrying out the evaluation.

Write the Structure that has the Internal Metrics.

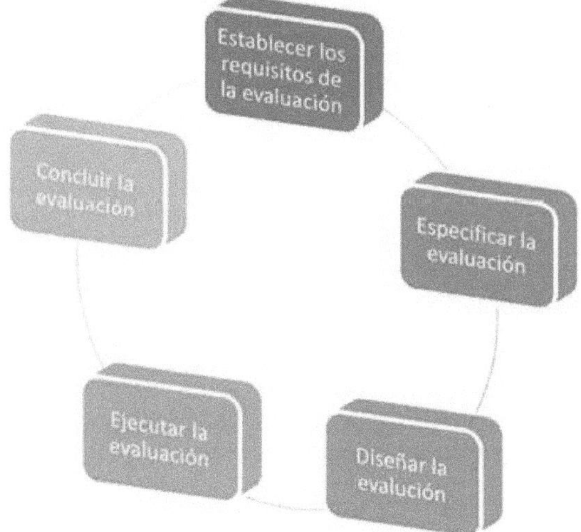

Permite al usuario iniciar
acciones correctivas
temprano en el ciclo del
desarrollo

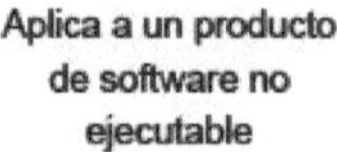

Aplica a un producto
de software no
ejecutable

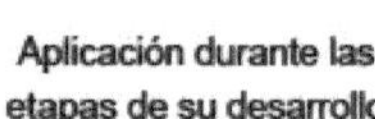

Permite predecir a
calidad del producto
final

Aplicación durante las
etapas de su desarrollo

Permiten medir la
calidad de los
entregables
intermedios

Allows the user to initiate corrective actions early in the cycle.
development
Applies to a non-executable software product
Allows to predict the quality of the final product
Implementation during the stages of its development
They allow the quality of intermediate deliverables to be measured.

Find in the following alphabet soup of the topic the key words as they are:

- Security
- Reliability
- Usability
- Mantebility
- Compatibility

4	5	6	7	8	9	10	11	12	13	14	15	16	17	18	19	20	21	22	23	24
25	26	27	28	29	30	31	32	33	34	35	36	37	38	39	40	41	42	43	44	45
46	47	48	49	50	51	52	53	54	55	56	57	58	59	60	61	62	63	64	65	66
67	68	69	70	71	72	73	74	75	76	77	78	79	80	81	82	83	84	85	86	87
88	89	90	91	92	93	94	95	96	97	98	99	100	101	102	103	104	105	106	107	108
109	110	111	112	113	114	115	116	117	118	119	120	121	122	123	124	125	126	127	128	129
130	131	132	133	134	135	136	137	138	139	140	141	142	143	144	145	146	147	148	149	150
151	152	153	154	155	156	157	158	159	160	161	162	163	164	165	166	167	168	169	170	171
172	173	174	175	176	177	178	179	180	181	182	183	184	185	186	187	188	189	190	191	192
193	194	195	196	197	198	199	200	201	202	203	204	205	206	207	208	209	210	211	212	213
214	215	216	217	218	219	220	221	222	223	224	225	226	227	228	229	230	231	232	233	234
235	236	237	238	239	240	241	242	243	244	245	246	247	248	249	250	251	252	253	254	255
256	257	258	259	260	261	262	263	264	265	266	267	268	269	270	271	272	273	274	275	276
277	278	279	280	281	282	283	284	285	286	287	288	289	290	291	292	293	294	295	296	297
298	299	300	301	302	303	304	305	306	307	308	309	310	311	312	313	314	315	316	317	318
319	320	321	322	323	324	325	326	327	328	329	330	331	332	333	334	335	336	337	338	339
340	341	342	343	344	345	346	347	348	349	350	351	352	353	354	355	356	357	358	359	360
361	362	363	364	365	366	367	368	369	370	371	372	373	374	375	376	377	378	379	380	381
382	383	384	385	386	387	388	389	390	391	392	393	394	395	396	397	398	399	400	401	402
403	404	405	406	407	408	409	410	411	412	413	414	415	416	417	418	419	420	421	422	423
424	425	426	427	428	429	430	431	432	433	434	435	436	437	438	439	440	441	442	443	444

Enter the Benefits of metric 25000.

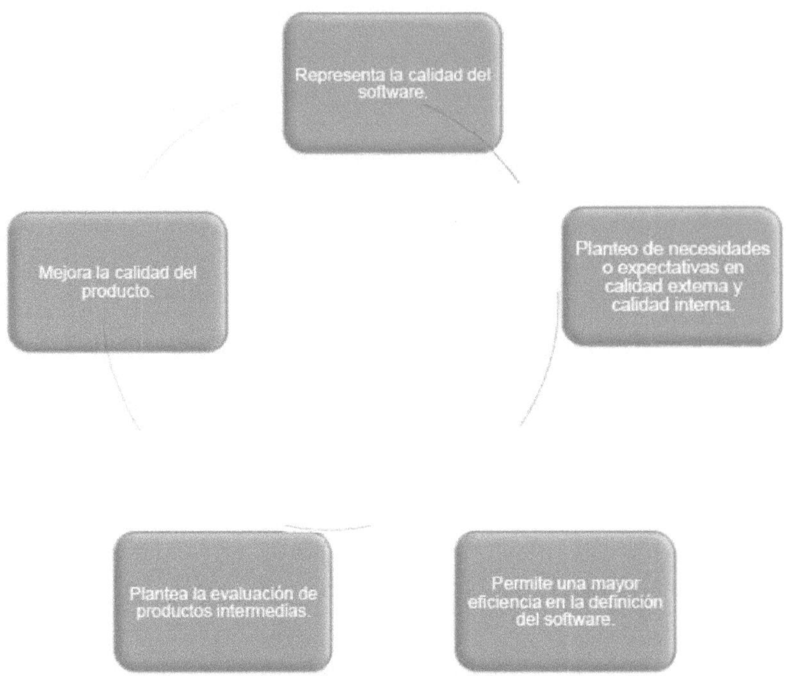

It represents the quality of the software.
Needs or expectations in terms of external and internal quality.
It allows for greater efficiency in software definition.
Improve the quality of the product.
It proposes the evaluation of intermediate products.

I EVALUATION

	FORMAT	SIMPLE
	CONTEXT	
	APPROACH	The ISO/IEC 25000 Standard is known as:
	OPTION A	It is known as AQuaRe (System and Software Quality Requirements and Evaluation).
	OPTION B	It is known *as a metric of software* being transported to the cloud.
1	OPTION C	It is known as the metric that describes the efficiency of the product.
	OPTION D	It is known as the QuaRe metric (Qualitu Requirements)
	RESPONSE CORRECT	A
	LEVEL	1

	OPERATION COGNITIVE	SIMPLE
2	FORMAT	SIMPLE
	CONTEXT	
	APPROACH	**ISO/IEC 25000 is the result of implementing what?**
	OPTION A	The above standards were implemented without specifying any
	OPTION B	Not implemented at all
	OPTION C	Only ISO/IEC 9126 and ISO/IEC 9126 were implemented. ISO/IEC 14598
	OPTION D	Previous standards were implemented, especially ISO/IEC 9126 and ISO/IEC 14598.
	RESPONSE CORRECT	D
	LEVEL	1
	OPERATION COGNITIVE	SIMPLE
3	FORMAT	SIMPLE
	CONTEXT	
	APPROACH	**What is the division of the ISO/IEC 25000 metric quality model?**
	OPTION A	• ISO/IEC 25010 (System and software quality models) This standard describes the quality of use of a given software. • ISO/IEC 25012.- (Data Quality Model). has a general model for data quality in an information system application.
	OPTION B	• ISO/IEC 25013.- (System and software quality models) This standard describes the quality of use of a given software. • ISO/IEC 25012 (Data Quality Model) has a general model for data quality in an information system application.
	OPTION C	• ISO/IEC 25011.- (System and software quality models) This standard describes the quality of use of a given software. • ISO/IEC 25015 (Data Quality Model) has a general model for data quality in an information system application.
	OPTION D	• ISO/IEC 25015 (System and software quality models) This standard describes the quality of use of a given software. • ISO/IEC 25006 (Data Quality Model) has a

		general model for data quality in application of a data quality management system.
		information.
	RESPONSE CORRECT	A
	LEVEL	1
	OPERATION COGNITIVE	SIMPLE
4	FORMAT	SIMPLE
	CONTEXT	
	APPROACH	**The following definition corresponds to** "(System and software quality models) This standard describes the quality of use of a given software".
	OPTION A	ISO/IEC 25016
	OPTION B	ISO/IEC 25012
	OPTION C	ISO/IEC 25006
	OPTION D	ISO/IEC 25010
	RESPONSE CORRECT	D
	LEVEL	1
	OPERATION COGNITIVE	SIMPLE
5	FORMAT	SIMPLE
	CONTEXT	
	APPROACH	**In ISO/IEC 2502 the division of quality measurement is composed of:**
	OPTION A	• ISO/IEC25020 . reference model and guide) provides guidance for users to develop and apply measures proposed as ISO standards. • ISO/IEC 25021.- (Quality measure elements) This metric does not recommend a set of metrics as a basis that can be used throughout the software lifecycle. • ISO/IEC 25023 (Measurement of system and software product quality) defines specifically the metrics to be used for software quality assessment. • ISO/IEC 25024 (Measurement of data quality): defines the metrics for the measurement of data quality.
	OPTION B	- ISO/IEC25020 . reference model and guide) provides a guide for users to develop and implement a

6		apply measures proposed as ISO standards. • ISO/IEC 25021.- (Quality measure elements) This metric does not recommend a set of metrics as a basis that can be used throughout the software lifecycle. • ISO/IEC 25022 (Measurement of quality in use) defines the metrics for software quality assessment. • ISO/IEC 25023 (Measurement of system and software product quality) defines specifically the metrics to be used for software quality assessment.
	OPTION C	• ISO/IEC25020 . reference model and guide) provides guidance for users to develop and apply measures proposed as ISO standards. • ISO/IEC 25021.- (Quality measure elements) This metric does not recommend a set of metrics as a basis that can be used throughout the software lifecycle. • ISO/IEC 25022.- (Measurement of quality in use) defines the metrics for the evaluation of software quallty • ISO/IEC 25023 (Measurement of system and software product quality) defines specifically the metrics to be used for software quality assessment. • ISO/IEC 25024 (Measurement of data quality): defines the metrics for the measurement of data quality.
	OPTION D	• ISO/IEC25020 . reference model and guide) provides guidance for users to develop and apply measures proposed as ISO standards. • ISO/IEC 25023 (Measurement of system and software product quality) defines specifically the metrics to be used for software quality assessment. • ISO/IEC 25024 (Measurement of data quality): defines the metrics for the measurement of data quality.
	RESPONSE CORRECT	C
	LEVEL	1
	OPERATION COGNITIVE	SIMPLE
	FORMAT	SIMPLE
6	CONTEXT	
	APPROACH	**The following definition corresponds to**

		"This standard is in charge of specifying the quality requirements that can be used in a software project we are developing".
	OPTION A	Division for the requirements of Quality (ISO/IEC 2503)
	OPTION B	Division for Quality Requirements.(ISO/IEC 2523)
	OPTION C	Division of the model for quality assessment (ISO/IEC 2504).
	OPTION D	Division of the model for quality assessment (ISO/IEC 2544).
	RESPONSE CORRECT	A
	LEVEL	1
	OPERATION COGNITIVE	SIMPLE
7	FORMAT	SIMPLE
	CONTEXT	
	APPROACH	**The following definition corresponds to** "This standard provides requirements and recommendations necessary to carry out the software product evaluation process".
	OPTION A	Division for the requirements of Quality (ISO/IEC 2503)
	OPTION B	Division for Quality Requirements.(ISO/IEC 2523)
	OPTION C	Division of the model for quality assessment (ISO/IEC 2504).
	OPTION D	Division of the model for quality assessment (ISO/IEC 2544).
	RESPONSE CORRECT	C
	LEVEL	1
	OPERATION COGNITIVE	SIMPLE
8	FORMAT	SIMPLE
	CONTEXT	
	APPROACH	**In ISO/IEC 2504 the division of the model for quality assessment is composed of:**
	OPTION A	• ISO/IEC 25040 (Evaluation reference model and guideline) provides a general reference model for the evaluation process. • ISO/IEC 25041 (Evaluation guide for developers, acquirers and independent evaluators) describes the requirements and recommendations

		for the implementation of a software product. • ISO/IEC 25043 (Evaluation module) defines the standard as evaluation module and documentation, structure and content to be included in the project documentation. • ISO/IEC 25044 (Evaluation module for recoverability) describes a single module with recoverability sub-characteristics.
	OPTION B	• ISO/IEC 25041 (Evaluation guide for developers, acquirers and independent evaluators) describes the requirements and recommendations for the implementation of a software product. • ISO/IEC 25042 (Evaluation module) defines the standard as evaluation module and documentation, structure and content to be included in the project documentation. • ISO/IEC 25045 (Evaluation module for recoverability) describes a single module with recoverability sub-characteristics.
	OPTION C	• ISO/IEC 25040 (Evaluation reference model and guideline) provides a general reference model for the evaluation process. • ISO/IEC 25041 (Evaluation guide for developers, acquirers and independent evaluators) describes the requirements and recommendations for the implementation of a software product. • ISO/IEC 25042.- (Evaluation module)
		defines the standard as an assessment and documentation module, structure and content to be included in the project documentation. - ISO/IEC 25044 (Evaluation module for recoverability) describes a single module with recoverability sub-characteristics.
	OPTION D	• ISO/IEC 25040 (Evaluation reference model and guideline) provides a general reference model for the evaluation process. • ISO/IEC 25041 (Evaluation guide for developers, acquirers and independent evaluators) describes the requirements and recommendations for the implementation of a software product. • ISO/IEC 25045 (Evaluation module for recoverability) describes a single module with recoverability sub-characteristics.
	RESPONSE CORRECT	C

	LEVEL	1
	OPERATION COGNITIVE	SIMPLE
9	FORMAT	SIMPLE
	CONTEXT	
	APPROACH	**What is the process to follow within ISO/IEC 25000 to carry out the assessment?**
	OPTION A	1. Establish the requirements of the evaluation 2. Designing the evaluation 3. Specify the evaluation 4. Execute the evaluation 5. Conclude the evaluation
	OPTION B	1. Establish the requirements of the evaluation 2. Specify the evaluation 3. Designing the evaluation 4. Execute the evaluation 5. Conclude the evaluation
	OPTION C	1. Establish the requirements of the evaluation 2. Specify the evaluation 3. Designing the evaluation 4. Execute the evaluation
	OPTION D	1. Establish the requirements of the evaluation 2. Designing the evaluation 3. Specify the evaluation 4. Execute the evaluation
	RESPONSE CORRECT	B
	LEVEL	1
	OPERATION COGNITIVE	SIMPLE
10	FORMAT	SIMPLE
	CONTEXT	
	APPROACH	**In establishing the purpose of the evaluation to be created.**
	OPTION A	A document is created which contains the purpose for which the organisation wants to assess the quality of its software product. (ensuring the quality of the product, deciding whether or not to accept a product, determine the viability of the project under development, compare the quality of the product with competing products, etc.).
	OPTION B	A document is created which contains the purpose for which the organisation wants to assess the

		reliability of its software product.
OPTION C		A document is created which contains the purpose for which the organisation wants to evaluate the usability of its software product.
OPTION D		A document is created which contains the purpose for which the organisation wants to evaluate the efficiency of its software product.
RESPONSE CORRECT		**A**
LEVEL		1
OPERATION COGNITIVE		**SIMPLE**

SOLUTION (EVALUATION)

1.   A) It is known as AQuaRe (System and Software Quality Requirements and Evaluation).

2.   D) Standards prior to this one, especially ISO/IEC 9126 and ISO/IEC 14598, were implemented.

3.   A)

o   ISO/IEC 25010 (System and software quality models) This standard describes the quality of use of a given piece of software.

o   ISO/IEC 25012 (Data Quality Model) has a general model for data quality in an information system application.

4.   (D) ISO/IEC 25006

5.   C)

o   ISO/IEC 25020 (Measurement reference model and guide) provides a guide for users to develop and apply measurements proposed as ISO standards.

o   ISO/IEC 25021.- (Quality measure elements) This metric does not recommend a set of metrics as a basis that can be used throughout the software lifecycle.

o   ISO/IEC 25022 (Measurement of quality in use) defines the metrics for software quality assessment.

o   ISO/IEC 25023 (Measurement of system and software product quality) defines specifically the metrics to be used for software quality assessment.

o   ISO/IEC 25024 (Measurement of data quality): defines the metrics for the measurement of data quality.

6.   A) Division for Quality Requirements (ISO/IEC 2503)

7.   C) Division of the Quality Assessment Model (ISO/IEC 2504)

8.   C)

o   ISO/IEC 25040 (Evaluation reference model and guideline) provides a general reference model for the evaluation process.

o   ISO/IEC 25041 (Evaluation guide for developers, acquirers and independent evaluators) describes the requirements and recommendations for the implementation of a software product.

o ISO/IEC 25042 (Evaluation module) defines the standard as evaluation module and documentation, structure and content to be included in the project documentation.

o ISO/IEC 25044 (Evaluation module for recoverability) describes a single module with recoverability sub-characteristics.

9. B)
a. Establish the requirements of the evaluation
b. Specify the evaluation
c. Designing the evaluation
d. Execute the evaluation
e. Conclude the evaluation

10. A) A document is created which contains the purpose for which the organisation wants to evaluate the quality of its software product (to ensure the quality of the product, to decide whether to accept a product, to determine the viability of the project under development, to compare the quality of the product with competing products, etc.).

CHAPTER III
Metrica 14598.

Competences

Identify the basic characteristics of Metric 14598 within what is involved in Software Engineering. Recognise the parameters offered by the metrics as a guide for an excellent software project.

Use of metrics In Software Engineering projects.

When you have read this unit the **learning outcomes**: Identify the characteristics of 14598 metrics that are used in different software projects.

You identify the processes involved and the benefit of the application of metrics. **Contents**

1.1 Research on Metric Issues 14598.

1.2 Features of Metrica 14598

Introduction

Currently many software developers have seen the need to control and evaluate the life cycle of software development, given this need metrics were implemented in the process of developing a software, the metrics are a fundamental part because they provide us with certain parameters or characteristics that help us to evaluate the quality and efficiency of a software.

Currently, there are many metrics that compare processes or software products to evaluate the quality, efficiency and design of a product, the metrics can be separated according to the size of the software, efficiency and quality. In the following, we will describe the functionalities and benefits of the 14598 metric in the field of software product evaluation.

3 Metrica 14598

Standard 14598, from the ISO/EC 9126 family of standards, arose in response to the need to define a set of characteristics that would take into account the purpose and use of the software and that would allow a valid model to be established for its subsequent evaluation.

3.1 Part 1

Three technical reports:

These reports should be for each process to be evaluated, for each possible solution to the possible problems that have emerged or obtained from the evaluation applied in the development of the system.

3.2 Part 2

Which gives the idea, of novelty:

This part deals with the idea that will help us to solve the problem posed by the person who commissions us to make a system, this idea is reflected in almost all the process, that is why this process must be evaluated, to see if the idea of solution has not been distorted, if we have not left the established in the requirements or if the person in charge is not comfortable with what we teach him, that is the reason why this metric must be applied.

The importance of this topic:

As we have already highlighted above, the importance of this topic is to find out if there is any possible flaw in the main idea of the system or if there **is a** lack **of** refinement of the system.

This part explains that the metric 14598, belongs to a family of ISO/IEC, so it has been well analysed and explained its purpose, since it belongs to something and it is not a rustic whole if not well defined this metric serves us at the time of evaluating a software, with all the parameters of quality and depending on the software that is being evaluated and the area to where it is directed, complying with all the standards of approval of the system.

Description of the content of the parts that make up the ISO/EC 9126 family of standards in which standard 14598 is immersed.

Part (1): The only one with a normative character so far, it describes a quality model for the software product, divided into two large blocks:

The standard or metric 14598 consists of the following parts, and has as its general title Information Technology - Software Product Evaluation:

Part 1: General Revision (ISO/IEC 14598-1)

Part 2: Planning and administration (ISO/IEC 14598-2)

Part 3: Process for Developers (ISO/IEC 14598-3)

Part 4: Process for Acquirers (ISO/IEC 14598-4)

Part 5: Process for assessors (ISO/IEC 14598-5)

Part 6: Documentation of Evaluation Modules (ISO/IEC 14598-6)

3.3 General Revision (14598-1).

Evaluation processes are not only involved in the evaluation of the quality of the software product, they also increase cost and time efficiency, the possibility in terms of human and monetary resources, trust and customer satisfaction.

Any software quality assessment process should start from a qualitative assessment, i.e. it should understand the attributes and qualities of the software and whether or not they meet the optimal requirements and standards to provide to a user.

This metric 14598 establishes 3 processes within the software quality assessment and they are:

* Developers' Process.
* Procurement Process
* Evaluator Process

3.3.1 Developers' process

ISO 14598 standards are generally used by organisations involved in the development of software products or the improvement of an already developed product, this evaluation process is done using all the established technical processes. It focuses on those indicators that can predict the quality of the final product, this process is done by measuring the indicators of the intermediate stages or processes of the software life cycle.

It provides a guide to clarify the quality requirements for carrying out the implementation and analysis of software quality measures.

It is applicable in all phases of the development life cycle. The standard itself is focused on the selection and reporting of some evaluation indicators in order to predict the quality of the final product by measuring the quality of intermediate products.

3.3.2 Procurement process

Within the 14598 standard, the procurement process is also involved. It should also be used by organisations or incorporated companies that are engaged in the development of software or in the improvement of existing software.

It can be applied to make a decision on the user's acceptance or satisfaction of a completed product, in order to proceed with a process of selecting the best product among several existing ones.

The ISO/IEC 14598 standard classifies software products into three groups:

* Commercial software products
* Existing software products developed or acquired by other organisations.
* Customised software products (bespoke software) or modified existing software products.

3.3.3 Evaluation process

Standard 14598 should be used by assessors carrying out an independent appraisal or evaluation of a software product. This appraisal or evaluation process may in some cases be performed at the request or suggestion of a developer, acquirer or others.

The evaluation process according to 14598 consists of four phases:

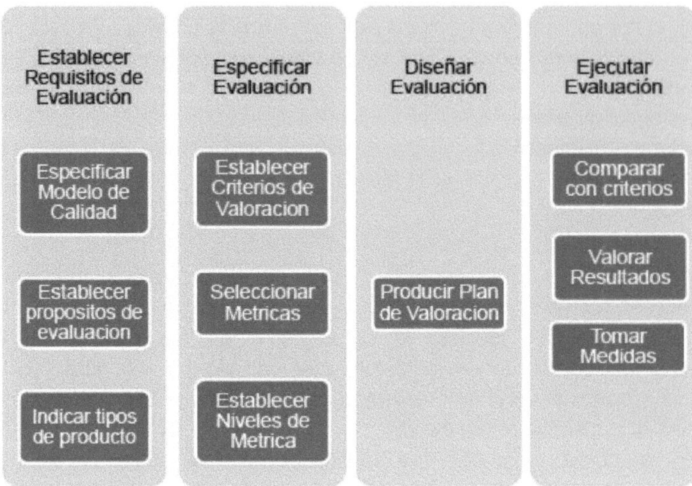

The standard can be used for:

Evaluate existing products

Evaluate products under development (in this case, the evaluation process must be synchronised with the development process).

3.4 ISO/IEC 14598 Assessment Process Characteristics

The characteristics pertaining to the evaluation process are as follows:

*   Repeatable
*   Reproducible
*   Impartial
*   Objective

3.4.1 Repeatable

Evaluation of the same software product with the same evaluation specification and performed by a different self-evaluator should produce results that can be accepted as identical.

3.4.2 Reproducible

The evaluation of the same software product with the same evaluation specification and performed by a different respective evaluator should result in a result of this process that can be accepted as identical.

3.4.3 Impartial

The respective evaluation should not only focus on any particular outcome, but can also be wrapped around different outcomes in order to achieve improvements in the quality of the development of the software product.

3.4.4 Objective

The results presented in the evaluation process must be truthful and verified to avoid inconveniences, citing an example not influenced by the feelings or opinions of the evaluator, but rather work ethically and morally.

3.5 ISO/IEC 14598 assessment process

The assessment process according to ISO/IEC 14598 comprises five sub-processes.
* Establishment of assessment requirements.
* Specification of the evaluation
* Evaluation Design
* Implementation of the Evaluation
* Conclusion of the Evaluation

3.6 Establishment of Requirements

The purpose is to describe the goal and objectives of the evaluation. Such goals relate to the use of the software product in consideration also of one or more user or customer viewpoints and the risks that may be associated with it, i.e. the evaluation requirements may actually focus on levels of evaluation for the same selected features or requirements.

3.7 Software Product Evaluation Process ISO/IEC 14598

Inputs	Phase of Evaluation	Key Tasks	Outputs
Product description, modulosdel product	Establish requirements of the evaluation	Establishment of assessment requirements	Evaluation requirements: describe the objectives of the evaluation, in particular describe quality requirements for the product.
Evaluation requirements, product description, pre-defined evaluation specifications	Specification of the evaluation	Specification of the assessment based on the assessment requirements and the description of the product of software provided by the applicant	The specification of the assessment defines the whole analysis and measuresa on the product and its components
Specification of the assessment,	Design of the evaluation	Design of the evaluation produces a	The evaluation plan focuses on the

description of the product, methods of evaluation		plan to evaluation on the basis of the evaluation specification, this activity takes into consideration all the components of product of the software to be evaluated	operational procedures involved in the evaluation process. specification of the the evaluation; in particular they describe all the methods and tools to be used in the evaluation
Plan evaluation, evaluation tools, product components	Implementation of the evaluation	Implementation of the evaluation consists of inspection, modelling. Measurement and testing of the product and its components according to the evaluation plan, these	The records of the evaluation are based on the plan for the evaluation, keeping an account of the detailsfrom actions taken by the
		activities can be carried out using software tools, the actions carried out by the evaluator are recorded and the results are obtained from positions in the draft evaluation report	evaluator, at how much executes the evaluation plan; these files are saved or stored by the evaluator. The draft set out in this section of the report of the evaluation carried out by the the evaluators is a document produced as a result of the synthesis of the evaluation results.
Draft evaluation plan, components of the	Conclusion of the evaluation	Conclusion of the evaluation which consists of the	The evaluation report will contain
product		delivery of the report of the evaluation of the productfrom software by part	requirements of the evaluation, the specification of the measures

			and
		of the evaluator as^ as well as their components when they have has been assessed independently	analysis realisedand any other information necessary to be able to repeat or reproduce the evaluation

3.8 Documentation of ISO/IEC 14598 Assessment Modules

This section of ISO/IEC 14598 sets out the structure and scope of the documentation of an evaluation module, i.e. in this case it is a format for the documentation of a module that is to carry out an evaluation.

The evaluation modules are used within the context of ISO/IEC 9126 and ISO/IEC 14598.

3.8.1 ISO/IEC 14598 Evaluation Module

This is an evaluation technology package for establishing measurements of software quality characteristics, sub-characteristics or attributes.

This package contains:

- Evaluation methods and techniques
- Inputs to the evaluation
- Collection of data to be measured
- Supporting procedures and tools.

3.8.2 ISO/IEC 14598 Assessment Instructions

This process describes in detail the procedure to be followed. This should also include what is the selection of evidence obtained by the group of evaluators, citing an example of the test code, the generation and recording of raw data, rules, computational algorithms for raw data metrics, the recording of results, and requirements for work retention and final documentation.

3.9 ISO/IEC 14598 Measurement Mapping

This item defines the meaning of the measurements, i.e. the interpretation of the results of the obtained measurements. This also includes what corresponds to an evaluation scale in which the obtained values are mapped by defined metrics. If several measures are obtained for a single characteristic, sub-characteristic or attribute then it must be defined how these can be combined into scores for characteristics, sub-characteristics or attributes within the software product to be evaluated.

3.10   Format for ISO/IEC 14598 Documentation

3.10.1 Foreword and Introduction
3.10.1.1 Foreword

It will provide information about:
- Preparation, approval, contributions and changes.
- Relation to other standards or other documents.

3.10.1.2 Introduction

It is a preamble or beginning of the priority techniques under the evaluation modules.

3.10.2 Scope

3.10.2.1 Features

Identifies characteristics, sub-characteristics or attributes for an evaluation module to be evaluated. The Quality model of ISO/IEC 9126-1 shall be used for the purposes of this clause.

3.10.2.2 Level of Assessment

This section should describe and specify the level of assessment to be benchmarked in an assessment module.

3.10.2.3 Techniques

Describes the evaluation techniques applied for an evaluation module. Citing as examples the growth models in terms of reliability, benchmarking, statistical analysis of code.

3.10.2.4 Applicability

Identifies the scope of the evaluation module evaluation within what is a software product, citing an example the evaluation module can be carried out on a particular programming language.

3.10.3 References

This section has as a fundamental part to provide references to standards and technical documents, if the software evaluation module depends on other modules it should be stated here.

3.10.4 Terms and Definitions

In this section you must establish the terms and conditions established within a module that is being evaluated.

These two metrics have established several standards in which they share criteria and characteristics, starting from the perspective of the evaluation process is based on a selected quality model, the standard ISO/IEC 14598 which means evaluation process, uses the quality model defined in ISO/IEC 9126 (quality model) and to perform the assessment of the characteristics, subcharacteristics and attributes that are given to a metric selection process determined in the second and third part of the metric ISO/IEC 9126.

They share a process of relationship also in terms of resources and environment that determines the process of product evaluation, this evaluation process either for developers,

The process is verified in the quality model 9126-1 and the assessment is carried out based on the internal and external metrics defined in ISO/IEC 9126-2 and ISO/IEC 9126-3 respectively. In conclusion, the evaluation process can be carried out on products that are currently in use, so that it will be based on the selected quality model and will be used for the assessment of the quality metrics in an ISO 9126/4 application.

3.12   Internal and External Quality: describes six characteristics

3.12.1 Functionality

This item is about the degree to which the software meets the needs indicated by the following list of attributes:

*   **Suitability:**

Suitability refers to the quality of being suitable. As such, it refers to the aptitude, willingness or ability that something or someone has for a particular purpose.

*   **Correction:**

Modification of a thing or person to correct its faults, errors, defects or imperfections.

*   **Compliance:**

Written or verbal consent or authorisation.

*   **Security:**

Absence of danger or risk.

*   **Reliability:**

Positive probability that a system or apparatus will perform a given function under certain conditions for a given time.

*   **Usability:**

Quality of the programme that are simple to use and easy to understand.

*   **Efficiency:**

Ability to perform or adequately perform a function.

*   **Maintainability:**

It is the property of a system that represents the amount of effort, in order to preserve its normal function or to substitute it.

- **Portability:**

Property that allows it to run on different platforms and operating systems.

All these sub-characteristics that manifest themselves externally during the use of the software as part of a system. They are the result of the internal attributes of the software.

As we can see the evaluation characteristics are 6, which has very well defined quality, as it consists of reliability; this part tells us that the product will be accurate, that it will not have any faults, that it has been reliable, and also reliability, this tells us that our product or software will be reliable in all its parts or modules.

Understood as the combined effect perceived by the user of the above six characteristics. On this occasion, the model is not developed at the sub-characteristic level.

As an example and to make the ideas a little more concrete, we will cite that the **specified source is not valid.**

"Efficiency", corresponding to the internal and external quality model, is divided into sub-characteristics:

- Temporal behaviour

- Use of resources

- Compliance

Critical Analysis

The three aforementioned characteristics tell us that the system or product will be optimised in all its aspects, in order to achieve in the evaluation of systems established by the metric a total conformity of the system on the part of the user.

3.12.2 Use

The quality model is used to evaluate the quality of the product, both software and the complete software (software + hardware on which it is installed). Specifically, it should serve as a framework when establishing the objectives we want to achieve, both in the final products and in the intermediate ones. **Source specified is not valid.**

The use is already the final process of the software, so it is established to evaluate absolutely everything, to evaluate all the objectives that have been achieved in the process of the software life.

3.13   ISO/IEC 14598 assessment

The ISO/IEC 9126 family of standards (software product quality) has been developed at the same time as the ISO/IEC 14598 family (software product evaluation). In fact, both families are the result of the extension of the first version of ISO/IEC 9126:1991.**source specified not valid.**

According to ISO 14598 it determines how to evaluate a product and gives requirements for the evaluation of its software.

3.14   Characteristics of the metric 14598

- 1.- Resource - Evaluation Support
- 2.- Process - Evaluation Support
- 3.- Product - Internal Metrics - External Metrics.
- 4.- Effect - Metrics in use.

The ISO/IEC 14598 standard includes the following editorial steps for its documentary exposition:

Overview (ISO/IEC): this is the part summarising the following five sections and outlining the review of the multimedia publishing product and the quality reference model.

The following topics are covered in this section:

1 The examination requirements are set out.
2 It details the examination.
3 The evaluation plan is carried out

This framework provides an overview of the other 5 parts and relates software product evaluation and the quality model defined in ISO 9126.

3.15 Planning and Management ISO/IEC 14598

The following events are planned and managed here:

1 Point of view from which they will start.
2 Objectives.
3 Select the technology to be used.
4 Divide up the work to be carried out.
5 Examine the product software.

This part contains the planning and management, requirements and guidelines for the support functions such as the approach and management for the evaluation of the software product.

3.16   ISO/IEC 14598 Developers Process

At this point, developers will follow the following process: realisation, approach, requirements of the software to be realised, the product is designed and realised. **Specified source not valid.**

This part provides the requirements and recommendations for the evolution of the software product when the evaluation is conducted in parallel with the development and is carried out by the developer.

3.17   ISO/IEC 14598 Comparators Process

This step corresponds to the customers who order the product and follow the following process: requirements, definition of the assessment, design of the assessment for its subsequent execution.

This section deals with the process for purchasers that provides requirements and recommendations for the evaluation of a customised commercial software product or modification of an existing product, performed to assure purchasers that it meets the expected requirements.

In this step the quality of the product, the requirements and outlines for the software testing of the multimedia publishing product are evaluated following the following process: traceability, results, problems, improvements and conclusions.

Refers to the process of evaluators being guided or recommended for the practical application of software product evaluation as the various parties seek to understand, accept and trust the results of the evaluation.

3.19   ISO/IEC 14598 Assessment Module

The last step is to carry out the examination by measuring the process created in the previous step and documenting it following the structure of the previous points with this outline:

1   Introduction:

in which an outline of the evaluation process to be carried out is provided.

2   Scope:

detailing the impact of the applications to be examined on the software with respect to support.

3   Entrance fees:

The tests to be carried out are listed here.

4   Results:

This section will set out the conclusions reached after examination. **Source specified not valid**.

This section deals with the documentation of the assessment modules, provides guidelines for the documentation of the assessment, these modules represent the specification of the quality model of the corresponding internal and external metrics to be applied to a particular assessment, includes assessment methods and techniques plus the actual measurements resulting from their application.

In addition to its different stages, a framework is established to evaluate the quality of the software products provided, in addition to the metrics we should know if we have maintained an order at the time of development, and if at each stage of development has been maintained or has been fulfilled satisfactorily, this stage and above all to know if the user really knows what he wants and if it has been possible to finish with each aspect that the user has asked us.

The metric has certain steps to follow, such as:

Firstly, as in all software development, we must establish the evaluation requirements where we must identify the purpose of the evaluation, with what purpose we evaluate each aspect that we have been evaluating, then we identify the type of product that we are going to evaluate, to specify the quality model to use, also as we have already highlighted above we must select the most appropriate metric for this evaluation process in this case the 14598 metric, establishing the characteristics of the same, to achieve a clear understanding of the criteria of the evaluation, then, having all that established, we must design the appropriate evaluation for what we are going to evaluate, whether it is a process or some modules, so that when we have finished or concluded the survey, we will have to take the right decisions to change for the better what we have to change, sharing criteria, between the people who carry out the work of the evaluation, so that we do not overlook any possible failure, and that after that we should evaluate the results, because in the next works we will have a guide of the possible failures that we have at the moment of evaluating some similar software or as a guide to evaluate another type of software.

In addition, we must highlight those who make up the standard or are in charge of carrying out the standard at the time of applying the metric, those in charge are

- Developers
- Acquirers
- Evaluators

The aforementioned, as we already know them, are what are immersed in the first stages of a software development, the acquirers are the user or customer, as they have the need or problem, which they want to optimise, then follows the developer, who executes these requirements and these are evaluated, redundantly, by the evaluators.

The activities that a developer carries out are the following, in the first place, he/she raises the requirements that are requested, this are sent or established by the client, then he/she defines the evaluation and orients the person who is evaluating in the improvements of the errors, managing the final result. From this work we obtain the orderly management, since everything is detailed adequately, the prevention of possible future modifications, or we refer to when the software is already finished and the client is not satisfied with some part of it and asks us for some kind of changes, leading to reanalyze everything carefully, also it is given the handling of confidentiality that only those that develop know of the system and the person that suggested it and finally it is due to take in account the place in which the software is going to work, since q is not going to do for nothing of the world to the same place in which it is developed, reason why generally the people do not count on an adequate system as far as computers.

ISO/IEC 14598 standards

In its different stages, it establishes a framework for evaluating the quality of software products and provides metrics and requirements for the evaluation process. Whether by parts, modules or the entire system.

In particular, it is used to apply the concepts described in ISO/IEC 9126. It defines and describes the activities necessary to analyse evaluation requirements, to specify, design and perform evaluation actions and to conclude the evaluation of any type of software product.

3.20 Characteristics ISO/IEC Standard 14598

The standard defines the main features of the assessment process:

1 Repeatability
2 Reproducibility.
3 Impartial
4 Objectivity

For these features the concrete measures involved are described

1 Analysis of the evaluation requirements:
in this part of the system, all the demands or requests are taken from the person requesting the optimisation of a problem or a need, such as a client or user, who is the one who generates the whole process of software development.

2 Evaluation of specifications:
in this part are evaluated each one of the aspect, so that there is no irregularity and do not exist the changes at the last moment, come to have some displeasure on the part of the person that us encargo to solve the problem, also is recommendable to carry out each one of these activities and informing to the user or client of the advances that go giving d^a to day, for as^ avoid any type of mishaps that can be presented at the time of delivering the product, avoiding the displeasure of the client and the double work of the people that are in charge of the creation of the software.

3 Evaluation of the design and definition of the evaluation plan:
In this part it is about how we are going to evaluate some process or module in general, that we are going to use for that software, for that tool which is the suitable one, and that if the process to evaluate is going to do the correct thing at the moment of being evaluated, this is wanted that each thing or step that is given, This is why the standards are established, in this case metric 14598, which is one of the families of metric 9126, which are the most appropriate and the ones we are studying for the evaluation of a system.

4 Implementation of the evaluation plan:
In this part, when we have already established the rules or the evaluation metrics, we proceed to execute it, taking into account the results of the part that we are evaluating, since it is obvious that we want to observe and analyse if what we are developing is right, so it is very important to compare the results with the requirements of the person who commissioned us the system, and if it is possible we should take a report and show it to that person so that he/she can also observe and be sure of what he/she is going to receive as a final product, because if failures occur in the evaluation and it is shown to the person who commissioned the system it is obvious that changes will be generated but only in the part where we are evaluating but not when we have finished all the work.

So^ we can highlight the good things, what is the point of analysing what we do and what benefits we get from the evaluation we carry out and to whom we benefit from the evaluation we apply.

5 Evaluation of the conclusion:
In this aspect as previously mentioned, the evaluation of conclusions is rather the correction of the errors found in the process that we are carrying out at the moment of evaluating this part of the system, this conclusion to make more precise the results obtained is advisable to share it with the person who commissioned us to carry out the system as previously mentioned.

This avoids numerous medications at the end of the system, making it a tedious task to implement them.

modifications. **Source specified not valid.**

3.21 Services ISO/IEC 14598 standard

Services related to the evaluation of software products are generally tailored to the measurements of individual end-users or suppliers, depending on why the evaluation was requested.

Software evaluation services include:

1 Definition of software reference quality profiles.
2 Assessment according to predefined quality models.
3 Software quality certification according to quality models and standards.
4 Comparisons between products.
5 Software re-engineering.
6 Services of product quality monitors. **Source specified not valid.**

1. **ESTABLISH REQUIREMENTS FOR THE EVALUATION**
2. **Establish evaluation purposes**
3. **Identify the types of products**
4. **Specify the quality model**
5. **SPECIFY THE EVALUATION**
6. **Select the metrics**
7. **Set levels for metrics**
8. **Establish assessment criteria**
9. **DESIGNING THE EVALUATION**
10. **Produce evaluation plan**
11. **TO CARRY OUT THE EVALUATION**

12. **Taking action**
13. **Compare with criteria**
14. **Assessing results**

The quality model is a series of forms that allow to manage all the information related to the quality model to be used in the evolution. In the first one, a quality model is created by defining its name, a description and the quality characteristics that compose it.

The second form allows the creation of quality characteristics that are included in the model. It defines the name, the type of characteristic it belongs to, i.e. a classification depending on the internal, external or in-use context where it is to be applied, a description and the related sub-quality characteristics.

3.22 Definition of Evaluation

This model consists of two forms. The first one allows to establish the products to be evaluated. Within the products to be evaluated, intermediate products such as data models or final products such as the executable file can be chosen.

The second form is divided into two parts. The first one establishes the requirements of the evaluation, in which the purpose, the audience, the intention, the name of the software, the objectives of the evaluation and those responsible for the evaluation are defined. The second part defines the specification of the evaluation, which defines the quality model, the characteristics, the sub-characteristics and the metrics that are going to be evaluated for each of the selected products. **Source specified not valid.**

The benefits offered by metrics in terms of product evaluation is the definition of quality benchmarks, evaluating predefined system modules, giving a quality certification according to quality standards, creating a comparison between software engineering products, having a product quality monitoring service.

It should also be noted that not only the staff who are developing the system benefits, but also the person in charge, as they get the system at the specified time and do not have to go through unnecessary inconvenience.

As we have already seen, from all the above already investigated, this metric is an evaluation guide, which has some requirements that must be followed according to the type of software that we are evaluating, produced by the standards of the ISO/IEC 14598, these standards are used by people in charge of maintenance to measure compliance with the requirements that have been given, to see if there are failures and make their respective improvements as it is evaluated, a something, to obtain improvements of that something, in this case a system - software, the same one that if in the evaluation, using the metric 14598, presents some inconsistency in the data or some process this generating some error, in its effect all that module will be changed or improved, since the program must be echo by modules, for as^ not to have to be spending the time revising all the code, unnecessarily, with this it is possible to emphasize that this norm is very useful since it is linked with the process of the ISO/IEC 9126, reason why its characteristics in the evaluation process are precise and very useful as we already said previously to evaluate the process with which the development of the software is being handled, as they are the repetitiveness, in this point it is analyzed and evaluates that some process is not generating some type of duplicate that has been repeated, then we have the reproducibility, this part focuses on what the user has asked us to do if it is correct, if it complies with what has been established, if the problem is solved, impartiality, that any data requested has been unique and accurate, and finally the objectivity that as the name says that it has been objective and is not being redundant in what is asked of the user. Complying with the standards mentioned above and broken down, allows us to have a degree of quality of the product because if it approves them, it reflects that the system is suitable and is useful in all its aspects, it should be noted that also in this standard evaluation work is done when the software is already installed on the respective computer to see if it really has any problems in the machine that will be used finally, since it can be very different the capacity of answer in the machine that is worked it that in the machine that is going to implement it, and can generate some type of improvisation causing some type of displeasure and inconformity with the user, in this way increases but the quality of evaluation if it fulfils all these requirements, this also serves to give him the value or cost of this software.

In the evaluation of the software we have noticed that it is very important to abide by the models and standards, these models and standards must be as updated as possible, as they must be updated to have a quality evaluation, as we have noticed a quality evaluation is nothing more than evaluating the process by which the system is going through and will be developed and as we said until the same installation in which it will be in the final computer, until that process is evaluated to observe if an error exists, a failure has been in system or out of it, for there are computers that the systems cannot be installed because they lack a complement or because they do not fulfil with everything on the installation so^ that it is debugging this type of failures by means of the evaluation in the metric 14598, because they detail the characteristics by means of which not only the evaluation of the metric is made but also of technical metrics of quality of the software that are the indicators. It is also necessary to take into account the scales of qualitative and quantitative measurement since it is possible and it is necessary to qualify the qualities of the software to have a greater acceptance and certain degree of satisfaction because it has fulfilled the characteristics that have been recommended, also the evaluation of the quantitative part must be given since the expenses of the software vary according to the necessities of one with another, and according to the external necessities that can be presented, these two characteristics to evaluate are very important as far as the evaluation of quality of the product or processes.

In order to be clear about software quality, two important concepts must be taken into account:

Quality:

According to the Rhae language, it is the priority or set of priorities inherent to something, which allow its value to be judged.

Software:

It is a set of programs, instructions and computer rules that allow different tasks to be executed on a computer. So it is defined, the 14598 metric, which as we already know defines software evaluation as a quality model to a set of characteristics and the relationship between them, which form the basis for specifying quality requirements and evaluating quality.

As we could observe the quality models offer the standards and parameters, which are expected for the creation of software projects. The quality of software is fundamental for a company and its evaluation becomes relevant in order to fulfil its purposes that are required to be achieved with the help of these software products.

With this we can say that every software evaluation model is important and that every quality model has sub-characteristic measurements.

3.24   Identification of the types of Products to be assessed

The identification of the product is to establish the type of product to be evaluated, if it is Base Software, citing an example, it can be System

Operational, it can also be Utility software, e.g. a CASE tool or some application software, e.g. security software, it can be financial or educational software.

Software Product Type	Example
Base Software	Operating System
Utility Software	Tool Case
Application Software	Educational Software

3.25   Designing the Evaluation

The evaluation plan describes the evaluation methods and the schedule of actions to be taken into account by the evaluator. The evaluator may act in a manner consistent with the measurement plan.

3.26   ISO/IEC 14598 Planning and Management

This section of the standard provides requirements, recommendations or suggestions and guidance for the support department which is in charge of managing the evaluation within the software product and the technology necessary for the evaluation of the software product.

Software Evaluation Activities:

DEVELOPED SOFTWARE		PURCHASED SOFTWARE	
Activities of Development	Activities of Evaluation	Activities of Acquisition	Activities of Evaluation
The deliverables depend on the election of the LIFE CYCLE (Specification of requirements, specification of the design of the system)	Evaluation of deliverables sperm (exits from the project) (Revision of the design system)	Depends on the selection of the processes of procurement (Process of Suppliers)	Revisionof outlets specific to the processes of acquisition. Audit of the processes of suppliers

Relationship between support department and evaluation project

SUPPORT DEPARTMENT PROVEE	DRAFT EVALUATION DEVELOP
New Technology	Project experience
Standards standardse international	Evaluation experience
Specialisation (consultancy)	Project data
Training	Experience with technology
Organisational database	Response to the support function
Support to evaluation projects	

When a company or organisation wishes to plan and carry out a software evaluation, the following steps should be followed:

• Define the objectives of the software evaluation.

• Ensure a quantitative evaluation plan for all projects to be evaluated, this plan can be divided into sub-plans in order to establish an optimal evaluation.

Organisations or companies can carry out software evaluations based on the following:

- Ensure that the results of the evaluation can be verified and certified.
- Ensure effective technology and best practice in use.
- Ensure that recommendations for future evaluation activities are available.

Bibliography

[1] V. Rosales Morales, G. Alor Hernandez, J. L. Garcia Alcaraz, R. Zatarain Cabada and M. Barron Estrada, "An analysis of tools for automatic software development and automatic code generation," *Revista Facultad de Ingenieria Universidad de Antioquia,* vol. 77, 2015.

[2] M. Estayno, G. Dapozo, L. Cuenca and C. Greiner, "Modelos y Metricas para evaluar calidad software. Greiner, "Modelos y Metricas para evaluar calidad de software", *XI Workshop of Researchers in Computer Science, 2009.*

[3] R. S. Pressman, Software Engineering: A Practical Approach, Sixth ed., Mexico: McGraw Hill, 2006.

[4] I. Sommerville, Ingenieria del Software, Septima ed., Mexico: Editorial Pearson, 2005.

[5] G. a. Ruiz, A. Pena and C. A. Castro, "Modelo de Evaluación de Calidad de SoftwareBasado en Logica Difusa, Aplicada a Metricas deUsabilidad de Acuerdo con la Norma ISO/IEC 9126," *Aavances en Sistemas e Informatica,* vol. 3, n° 2, pp. 25-29, 2006.

[6] L. Perurena and M. Moraguez, "Usability of websites, methods and techniques for evaluation," *Revista Cubana de Informacion en Ciencias de la Salud,* vol. 24, n° 2, pp. 176-194, 2013.

[7] M. A. Abud Figueroa, "Quality in the Software Industry. La Norma ISO- 9126," *revistaupiicsa,* 2012.

[8] C. A. Largo Garrta and E. Marin Mazo, "Guia Tecnica para evaluacion de software," [On-line]. Available: https://jrvargas.files.wordpress.com/2009/03/guia_tecnica_para_evaluacion _of_software.pdf. [Last accessed: 27 July 2018].

[9] A. Holzinger, G. Searle and A. Nischelwitzer, "On Some Aspects of Improving Mobile Applications for the Elderly," from *International Conference on Universal Access in Human-Computer Interaction,* 2007.

[10] R. Harrison, D. Flood and D. Duce, "[Usability of mobile applications: literature 0] review and rationale for a new usability model," *Journal of Interaction Science,* vol. 1, n° 1,2013.

[11] J. Enriquez and S. Casas, "Usability in mobile applications," *ICT-UNPA,* 1] 2013.

Printed by Books on Demand GmbH, Norderstedt / Germany